The Drawer Book

A Comprehensive Guide for Woodworkers

 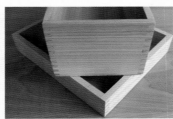 

BILL HYLTON

POPULAR WOODWORKING BOOKS
CINCINNATI, OHIO
www.popularwoodworking.com

Read This Important Safety Notice

To prevent accidents, keep safety in mind while you work. Use the safety guards installed on power equipment — they are for your protection.

When working on power equipment, keep fingers away from saw blades, wear safety goggles to prevent injuries from flying wood chips and sawdust, wear hearing protection and consider installing a dust vacuum to reduce the amount of airborne sawdust in your woodshop.

Don't wear loose clothing, such as neckties or shirts with loose sleeves, or jewelry, such as rings, necklaces or bracelets, when working on power equipment. Tie back long hair to prevent it from getting caught in your equipment.

People who are sensitive to certain chemicals should check the chemical content of any product before using it.

Due to the variability of local conditions, construction materials, skill levels, etc., neither the author nor *Popular Woodworking* books assumes any responsibility for any accidents, injuries, damages or other losses incurred resulting from the information presented in this book.

The authors and editors who compiled this book have tried to make the contents as accurate and correct as possible. Plans, illustrations, photographs and text have been carefully checked. All instructions, plans and projects should be carefully read, studied and understood before beginning construction.

Prices listed for supplies and equipment were current at the time of publication and are subject to change.

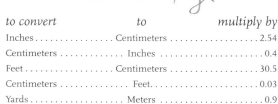

684.104
Hyl

Metric Conversion Chart

to convert	to	multiply by
Inches	Centimeters	2.54
Centimeters	Inches	0.4
Feet	Centimeters	30.5
Centimeters	Feet	0.03
Yards	Meters	0.9
Meters	Yards	1.1

Distributed in Canada by Fraser Direct
100 Armstrong Avenue
Georgetown, Ontario L7G 5S4
Canada

Distributed in the U.K. and Europe by David & Charles
Brunel House
Newton Abbot
Devon TQ12 4PU
England
Tel: (+44) 1626 323200
Fax: (+44) 1626 323319
E-mail: postmaster@davidandcharles.co.uk

Distributed in Australia by Capricorn Link
P.O. Box 704
Windsor, NSW 2756
Australia

Visit our Web site at www.popularwoodworking.com or our consumer Web site at www.fwbookstore.com for more woodworking information and other arts and crafts projects.

Other fine Popular Woodworking Books are available from your local bookstore or direct from the publisher.

13   12   11   10   09   5   4   3   2   1

Library of Congress Cataloging-in-Publication Data

Hylton, William H.
  The drawer book / by Bill Hylton. -- 1st ed.
     p. cm.
  ISBN 978-1-55870-842-6 (hardcover : alk. paper)
  1. Furniture making--Amateurs' manuals 2. Storage in the home--Amateurs' manuals. I. Title.
  TT195.H96 2009
  684.1'04--dc22

                        2009002671

ACQUISITIONS EDITOR: David Thiel, david.thiel@fwmedia.com
SENIOR EDITOR: Jim Stack, jim.stack@fwmedia.com
DESIGNER: Brian Roeth
PRODUCTION COORDINATOR: Mark Griffin
PHOTOGRAPHER: Bill Hylton
ILLUSTRATORS: Bill Hylton and Jim Stack

fw media

About the Author

Bill Hylton is a longtime woodworker and writer, best known for his router books. *Woodworking with the Router* and *Router Magic*. His other books include *Illustrated Cabinetmaking*, and two Popular Woodworking titles, *Bill Hylton's Power Tool Joinery* and *Bill Hylton's Frame & Panel Magic*. He is a frequent contributor to *Woodworker's Journal* magazine.

TABLE OF CONTENTS

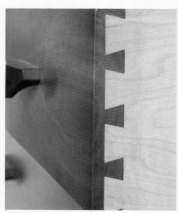

INTRODUCTION

Drifting into a custom furniture-maker's booth at the Philadelphia Furniture Show a few years ago, I slowly opened, then closed, then reopened a drawer in one of the display pieces. "You must be a woodworker," said the lady standing by (the craftsman's wife, as it turned out). "No one else looks at drawers like that. Just woodworkers."

And it's true, of course. The construction and fit of the drawers in the projects we make are key indicators of just how good we are as craftsmen. The choice of materials and hardware, the craft reflected in the joinery, the fit of the drawer in its pocket, and the ease and precision of its movement all speak volumes about the skill of the maker.

Consequently, no other aspect of furniture making draws such immediate attention from the craft's practitioners and aficionados. Or causes as much anxiety in woodworkers. Mastery requires careful work and lots of practice, but plain old know-how is essential. The know-how is in this book.

I approached this project in my usual way, digging into every aspect of the subject I could think of: Designs new and old, ways in which drawers are incorporated into furniture, materials used to build them, joinery, fitting techniques and more. With my head packed with info and ideas, I withdrew to the shop and tried it all.

Months later, having completed the text, more than 500 photos, and nearly 65 drawings for this book, I'm contemplating — at last!, — a schedule for completing a sideboard, a credenza, two small chests, a full chest of drawers and a couple of shop cabinets. All appear in the book, though not in their entirety. Each needs work — a couple of more drawers, a base, a top or a back. And, of course, all need finish.

I started these pieces as photo props, so I could show how drawers relate to and mount in different types of cases — from traditional solid-wood chests with drawer dividers,

runners, guides, and stops, to cases with drawers on side-mounted runners and cases with wide drawers guided by center-mounted slides, and on to contemporary cabinetry with drawers on mechanical slides. You build of it what you must, get the photos you need, and move on. The piece abides.

These pieces further served as props for photos showing many different drawer configurations and constructions and how, step-by-step, you cut the parts, cut the joinery, assemble the drawers, and fit them to the case.

No one drawer design or construction method is universal. The demands on drawers in the kitchen are different than those on drawers in the bedroom. Our expectations for each are different too. How you meet the demands within your expectations doubtless differs from how other woodworkers do it. Moreover, woodworking skills and tooling and access to materials vary.

With this in mind, I show you how to select an appropriate species for making drawers,

and how to prepare it for use, focusing on several ways of resawing stock. But I also cover plywood and other sheet goods, including ways to edge-band them.

Cutting joints suited for drawer construction is shown in step-by-step detail. The range includes everything from fastened butt joints and pocket screws through sawed and routed lock joints to both through hand-cut and machine-cut and half-blind dovetails.

The closing chapter pulls all this know-how together and shows you how to build and properly fit a drawer for an heirloom or for a practical kitchen.

Whether you're a novice looking for basic how-to or a practiced hand looking for different approaches to try, I think you'll find practical, useful information here on all aspects of drawer-making. You want to be ready when that curious woodworker slides a drawer open in your shop or home, right?

CHAPTER ONE

Drawer-building Basics

Drawers are built into all sorts of furniture. Not only chests of drawers, sideboards, cabinets, desks and cupboards, but into tables, even chairs and under beds. Woodworkers have put drawers inside lidded chests, and drawers inside drawers.

Each drawer is an open-topped storage container. Just a box. Function doesn't require a drawer to be fancy or complicated. Typically, we make them of a bland wood, selected because it's cheap, with just the front made to match (or complement) the furniture piece itself. But we want them to be sturdy and tight, probably not too heavy and easy to open and close.

If you are a furniture maker, you want it to be something you can construct quickly without sacrificing strength and durability or appearance. This is a bigger challenge than it might appear.

A drawer arguably receives more punishment than any other furniture component. You jerk it open. You slam it shut. Open. Bang! Shut. Open. Bang! Shut.

A strong, long-lasting drawer not only needs good joinery, but also a good method of supporting it in a chest and guiding its movement. If it sticks in the case and you need to jerk on it to get it to move, you put extra stress on the joints between the front and the sides. (And you stress the chest itself too.) If you have to throw a hip against it to get it to close, you again are putting extra stress on the drawer's and the chest's joints.

Traditionally, drawers are constructed and fitted with a lot of hand work. In an article on "the classical method" of making a drawer, Ian Kirby pointed out that "it's neither quick nor easy — nor is it cheap: You have to allow about a day of bench work per drawer. It's too rich for many applications. The fitted solid-wood drawer is a luxury for your finest work."

But time is dear. The hobbyist is juggling a day job and family responsibilities, blocking out a few hours here and there for woodworking. The professional has to make every expensive minute productive. So most contemporary woodworkers favor machine-cut joinery and easy fits.

There is, it turns out, no one way to build a drawer.

Parts of a Drawer

Every drawer has the same basic parts: front, back, side and bottom. But you can size and assemble them in a variety ways to produce different types of drawers. Curiously, it's not how the drawer is constructed so much as how its front relates to the case that gives the drawer type its name.

The *flush* drawer is easily the most common type used in furniture. The drawer front is set in the case so its face is flush with the case facade. To look right, with an even gap all around, the drawer has to be right. Moreover, in a chest of drawers, it has to match its neighbors. All need to be flush, all need to have the same visual clearance all around. This makes it the least forgiving type for the craftsman.

The *lipped* drawer has a rabbet on the inside edges of its front. The front thus nestles partway into the case with the lip covering the gap between the drawer front and the case. The benefit is that the lip covers up a loose fit — how practical is that!

The rabbet is cut on at least the side and top edges, and sometimes on the bottom edge as well. More often than not, the lip is profiled with a bead.

The *overlay* drawer's front overlays the edges of the case, concealing it. Often — but not always — the front is an element distinct from the drawer box, one attached after the box is assembled. It may be attached with adjusters; eccentrics that allow the front to be shifted up or down, side to side, or even cocked slightly. With this style, the drawer builder can deal with alignment by adjusting the front — not the entire box and its support system.

Regardless of type, the drawer front is usually made of the primary wood used in the chest. In any of the constructions, it can be an integral part of the drawer box, or added on — what's often called a false, show or applied front.

Drawer Parts:

1. Front   4. Bottom
2. Side   5. Slip
3. Back   6. Pull

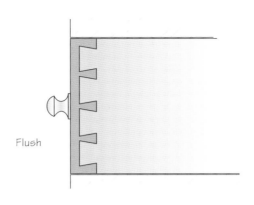

Flush

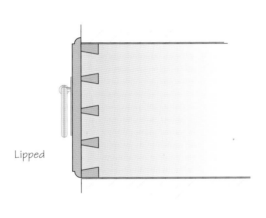

Lipped

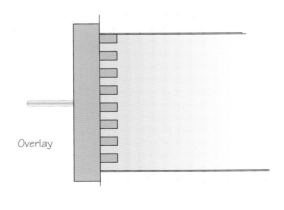

Overlay

Sides and Back

The drawer sides do a lot of work. Together with the front and back, they form the walls of the drawer box. Usually the sides provide the main support for the bottom, either directly or through slips that are glued to them.

In traditional drawer systems, the sides support the whole drawer as well, since its weight is transferred through the bottom edges to the runners that are built into the chest, cabinet or table. And there's more. The sides play vital roles in the drawer's movement. Those bottom edges are the bearing surfaces on which the drawer moves. The outer faces of the sides are the guides that rub against the chest walls, hopefully keeping the drawer on a straight course.

The back, on the other hand, does little beyond connecting the sides and enclosing the drawer box. In the typical traditional drawer, the bottom is secured to the back to keep it in place and keep it from sagging in the middle.

When the drawer moves, the back just rides along. In some designs, not only is the back set on top of the drawer bottom so it doesn't drag on the runners, it is deliberately held below the top edges of the sides so it doesn't drag on the overhead runners.

Primary-secondary matches can be complementary. This walnut-fronted drawer has butternut sides.

A drawer made of thin stock (top) just looks better than a comparable drawer made of stouter stock (bottom). Without sacrificing strength, the svelte drawer is lighter in weight.

Color contrast between the front and the sides is common, but it's usually lighter-colored sides of poplar or maple, matched (as shown above) with a darker cherry front.

Whether the back is flush with the ends of the sides (ABOVE LEFT) or recessed an inch or so (ABOVE RIGHT) is the builder's choice. Unless the drawer is mounted on full-extension slides, the back won't clear the case (except when it's completely removed). Is an extra inch of inside space important? It's your call.

Side-hung drawers have grooves in their sides to fit onto runners mounted in the case. The side must be thick enough to retain its structural integrity in spite of the grooves.

Cutting the back so it's a fraction of an inch below the top edges of the sides keeps it from dragging on the web frame above. Just a little less friction.

Bottom

As with drawer fronts, there are several types of drawer-bottom construction. Which you use depends on the material, the style of the drawer and whatever it's housed in, as well as the size of the drawer and how strong it needs to be.

A primitive type is the overlay construction. The bottom is simply laid over the edges of the sides, front and back and nailed. The durability and wear-ability of the construction are questionable. You'd think, for example, that wood movement would split the bottom or even break the joints. But some very old pieces — now in museums — have drawers built this way.

Moreover, the approach is making a comeback in low-end kitchen cabinetry. Especially in middle- to low-end cabinetry, in which the drawers are made entirely of melamine-coated particleboard and ride on bottom-mounted slides, the entire thing is slapped together very quickly with glue and staples.

Most common is the open-back construction, in which the bottom slides under the drawer back in grooves plowed in the drawer sides and front. This construction is essential if you plan to use a solid-wood bottom.

Open-back construction has several practical benefits. First, you can assemble the drawer box and fit it precisely to its housing before sliding the bottom in place. (In chapter 5, we'll see how this works.) Second, years from now, the bottom can be pulled out to facilitate a repair to the drawer.

The advent of effectively stable materials — plywood and hardboard, specifically — made the fully enclosed construction reasonable. Here the bottom is housed in grooves in the back as well as the sides and front. The bottom must be installed as the drawer is assembled, of course, and it's often glued in place. That strengthens and stiffens the structure, but makes it darn near impossible to modify or repair.

An interesting, yet uncommon, hybrid is the NK (developed in the early 1900s by Swedish Manufacturer Nordiska Kompaniet) construction. This bottom is composed of two runners and a bottom panel. It is assembled and fitted to the chest, and then the drawer box is glued to it. It's easy to fit and have the drawer track perfectly.

NK construction involves a different routine for building a drawer and fitting it to the case. The bottom and runners are fitted to the drawer pocket (LEFT); it's easier to do this than to fit an entire drawer to the pocket. Then the bottom assembly is joined to the drawer box (BELOW LEFT).

By far the most common bottom construction features a 1/4" plywood panel housed in grooves cut into the drawer sides and front. When combined with an open back, the bottom can be inserted after the drawer has been fitted to the case.

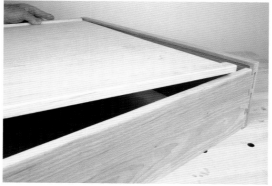

Bottom Constructions

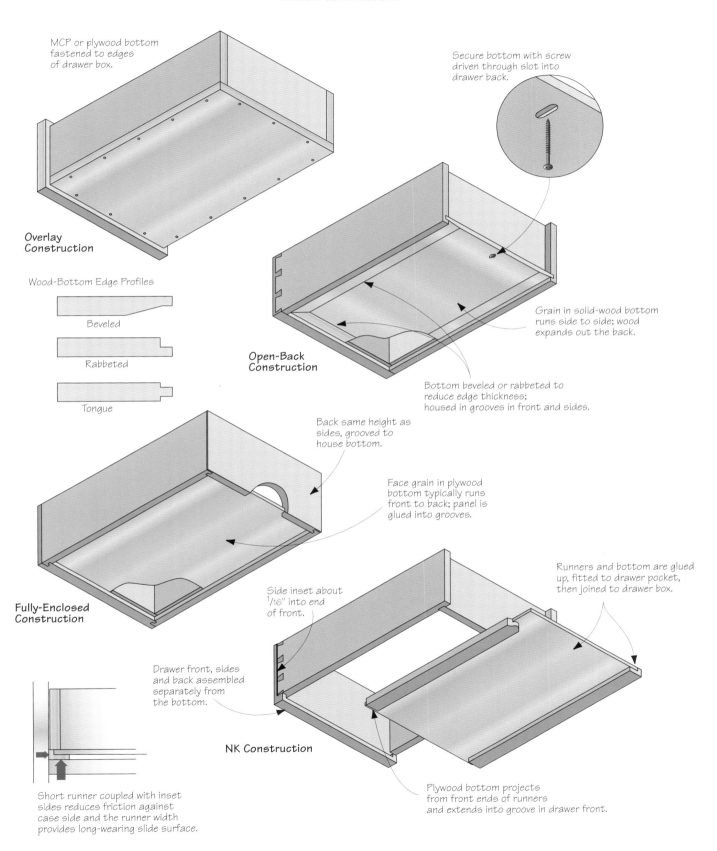

MCP or plywood bottom
fastened to edges
of drawer box.

**Overlay
Construction**

Wood-Bottom Edge Profiles

Beveled

Rabbeted

Tongue

Secure bottom with screw
driven through slot into
drawer back.

**Open-Back
Construction**

Grain in solid-wood bottom
runs side to side; wood
expands out the back.

Bottom beveled or rabbeted to
reduce edge thickness;
housed in grooves in front and sides.

Back same height as
sides, grooved to
house bottom.

Face grain in plywood
bottom typically runs
front to back; panel is
glued into grooves.

**Fully-Enclosed
Construction**

Side inset about
1/16" into end
of front.

Runners and bottom are glued
up, fitted to drawer pocket,
then joined to drawer box.

Drawer front, sides
and back assembled
separately from
the bottom.

NK Construction

Short runner coupled with inset
sides reduces friction against
case side and the runner width
provides long-wearing slide surface.

Plywood bottom projects
from front ends of runners
and extends into groove in drawer front.

Materials

Woodworkers are accustomed to the idea of making drawers from an assortment of materials.

The front is the primary wood, of course. But rarely are the sides and back made from the primary wood. We know we can save a little money using a less spectacular, less costly wood for the drawer sides and backs. We use this secondary wood for all the seldom-seen parts in a chest. In some contemporary chests, the drawer sides and backs (and structural fronts) are cut from plywood.

Then there's the bottom. It's traditional to make drawer bottoms from thin pieces of the secondary stock. But these days, plywood is used for the drawer bottoms more often than not. It's strong and light-weight. It's inexpensive and quick: You can transform a sheet of plywood into a stack of drawer bottoms in a matter of minutes. (You can buy it with a finish already applied, saving more time.)

In chapter 3: Choosing Materials, I'll delve into the criteria for selecting drawer-making materials (beyond the front). These include strength and weight, stability and wear-ability, aesthetics and reasonable cost.

Wood is usually the first choice for constructing drawers. Making the boards for a typical drawer box begins with rough-sawn 5/4 stock that's resawn into thinner, but still rough stock, then jointed and planed, ready for use.

A sheet of plywood can be reduced to a stack of drawer parts in a matter of minutes.

1. Primary Wood
2. Plywood
3. Secondary Wood

Constructions

Everybody likes to open drawers and see what's inside. But woodworkers usually look at the joints first, and maybe slide the drawer in and out a couple of times to gauge its fit in the case and the smoothness of its action. And then they'll look at the contents.

Such assessments reveal the aspects you need to keep in mind as you select the joints and constructions you'll use in building drawers for a particular chest. Looks are important.

All sorts of joints are used in drawers, from the traditional dovetail to the nailed butt. In my mind, the strongest joint needs to be between the front and sides. This is where the stress hits, every time a drawer is opened or closed. Also, this is the joint that needs to look good, because it is the one that's seen each time the drawer is opened.

The joint between the sides and back needs to be strong too, of course. But most of the stresses on it are second-hand, more inertial than direct. It's seldom seen, since you have to completely remove the drawer from the case to look at it. Here, in other words, function is more important than looks.

When you choose the joinery for a drawer project, you weigh a variety of considerations.
- The intent of the drawer
- The materials that will be used
- The mounting system
- Your woodworking skills
- The tools at your disposal
- The time available for construction

And you surely consider joint strength. We all have notions about the relative strengths of various joints. The generally accepted wisdom is that dovetail joints are the absolute best and strongest for drawers. But there are lots of possibilities, and lots of woodworking banter on the merits of each.

Traditional Drawer Construction
1. Integral Front
2. Solid-wood bottom
3. Half-blind dovetails
4. Through dovetails
5. Slip

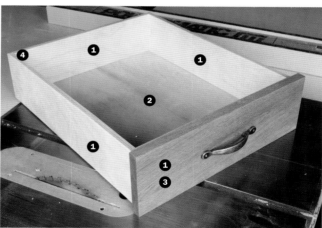

Contemporary Drawer Construction
1. Plywood front, sides and back
2. Plywood bottom
3. Applied front
4. Simple, machine-cut joinery

Front-to-Side Joinery

The front-to-side joints take the bulk of the strain on a drawer, and with a badly-built drawer, you can come away with just the drawer front in your hand. The drawings show most, if not all, of the practical options.

At one end of the drawer joinery spectrum, you have rudimentary fastened *butt joints* and their ilk. At the other are traditional dovetails, either machine-cut or hand-cut.

The woodworker's instinct (or is it conditioning?) is to cringe at butt joints, yet fastened butt joints — and I'd fold *pocket-screw joinery* into this clan — are widely used in drawers. Sometimes the joints aren't even glued. Much as we hate to acknowledge it, such joinery can hold up for decades — if not used hard.

Typically, the drawer's front and back are captured between the sides, with the fasteners oriented so they're perpendicular to the pull-push stresses. This exposes the sides' end grain to the front, of course, so an applied front is essential (unless looks don't count).

Closely related to the fastened butt joint is the *biscuit joint*, in which fasteners are supplanted by thin beech wafers. Biscuit joinery often is used in built-in cabinetry, so extending its use into the drawer boxes for the cabinets is logical. An applied front is needed to conceal the end grain of the drawer sides.

Biscuit joints are just fine for building drawer boxes that will have applied fronts. It's a natural choice for a cabinet being built of sheet goods using biscuit joinery. In your initial setup, be sure to choose a biscuit suitable for the stock thickness. The slot for a #20 biscuit will cut through ½"-thick material.

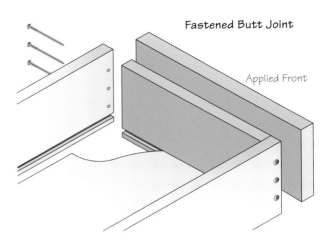

Fastened Butt Joint

Applied Front

Assembling a drawer box with butt joints is crude, but quick and reasonably effective. Brads or finish nails — or better, staples — can be pneumatically fired into the joint and virtually disappear. Screws, tailored to the material, need pilot holes but can draw the joint closed and resist withdrawal better than other fasteners. An applied front fixes the appearance.

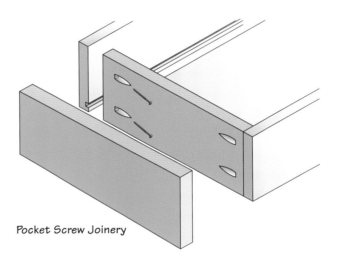

Pocket Screw Joinery

The difference between this and a fastened butt joint goes beyond the location and penetration angle of the screws. Here the screw angles into the long grain rather than penetrating the end grain. If you locate the screw pockets on the side's inner face, you can use this joint to attach a flush or lipped front.

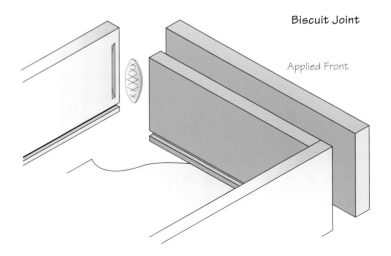

Biscuit Joint

Applied Front

The advantage of a plain *rabbet* or *dado* for joining a drawer front to the sides is ease of construction. Only one of the mating parts needs to be cut. Neither joint has any integral interlock, and there are no ideal long-grain-to-long-grain gluing surfaces, so you shouldn't expect the drawer to survive for generations.

A *rabbet-joint* variation is cut with a *dovetail* bit. Both mating parts must be machined, but the joint can be configured as a *halving* joint, in which both parts are cut with the same setup, albeit in different orientations.

Where construction efficiency is paramount, the *lock joints* are worth serious consideration. There are quite a few you can choose from, all with some form of parts interlocking to make assembly easier (but not eliminate the need for clamping, unfortunately). All have expanded glue area. All can be cut on the router table, some on the shaper and a few on the table saw. All work equally well on overlay and flush drawers and can be used to produce lipped drawers as well.

The most straightforward *locking joint* is a hybrid of the *dado and the rabbet joints.* It's easy to make, though it requires two different setups. It exposes the end-grain of the drawer side to the front of the drawer, so it needs a false front for all but the most utilitarian applications.

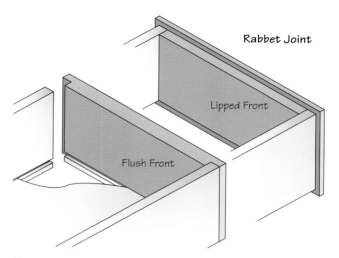

The rabbet joint has a lot of advantages as a drawer joint. It's easy to cut in a variety of ways, it's easy to assemble (reinforce it with nails, staples, screws, or dowels), reasonably strong, and not so unattractive that you want to hide it. The structural front doubles as the show front, saving material, and allows you to make either flush or lipped configurations.

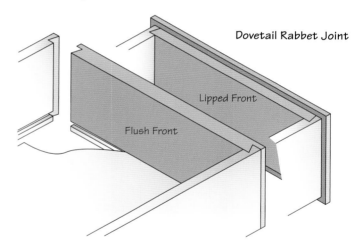

Though unsubstantiated by any test, I perceive the dovetail rabbet to be slightly stronger than a plain rabbet joint, thanks to the slightly angled faces. Cut it quickly on the router table as a *halving joint* and glue up with or without reinforcing fasteners or dowels. The front is integral to the box and can be configured as flush or lipped.

A dado can join front and sides in a drawer, but it isn't prime joinery. The joint won't resist the dominant stress — tension — put on drawers. The joint requires overhang on either end of the front, and that suggests mounting the drawer on mechanical slides, which will dramatically moderate the push-pull stress.

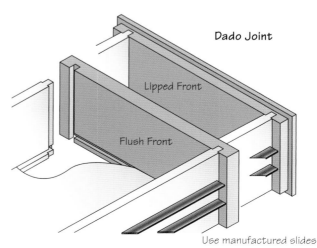

But transform the rabbet — so it's not a rabbet anymore — to create a short tongue for the dado, and a long one to overlap the end of the dadoed piece and you have a locking joint that doesn't need an applied front to be presentable. This is what's traditionally called a lock joint, though some folks call a *blind dado-and-rabbet joint*.

Like the standard dado-and-rabbet joint, the success of this lock joint hinges on the fit of the tongue in the dado. But it also requires the dado to be properly positioned, so the longer tongue contacts the end of the dadoed piece. You can cut this joint on either the table saw or the router table. There are no specific proportions or dimensions; just cut the dadoes and tongue to fit.

Easier to make is a *router drawer lock*. It's cut on the router table with a special router bit, so one cut dimension serves all constructions, regardless of stock thicknesses. The drawer side is run through standing on end against the fence, the front flat on the table. While it is often used to construct plywood boxes that get applied fronts, you can make flush and lipped drawers with it.

A variant is what I call a *drawer glue joint*, since you cut it with a down-sized glue-joint router bit. The profile is a little different, with extra shoulders. As with the more familiar drawer-lock bit, you do the cutting on a router table, sides on end against the fence and the front flat on the table.

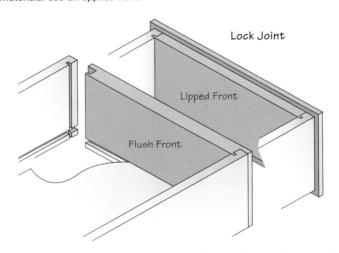

Dado-and-Rabbet Joint

Applied Front

By combining a dado cut and a rabbet cut to form one joint, you produce a mechanical interlock for a joint stronger than either cut alone. The weak spot in the joint is the long-grain shoulder between the side's butt end and the dado; the wider you make it — by using a thin tongue — the better. Suitable for all materials. Use an applied front.

Lock Joint

Lipped Front

Flush Front

The lock joint evolved from the dado-and-rabbet, no doubt (and was transformed by a tooling designer into shaper/router-cut lock joint). Cut it on the table saw or the router table and glue it up — no fasteners required. The show front becomes integral to the box; you can produce both flush and lipped configurations.

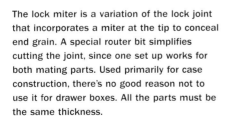

The lock miter is a variation of the lock joint that incorporates a miter at the tip to conceal end grain. A special router bit simplifies cutting the joint, since one set up works for both mating parts. Used primarily for case construction, there's no good reason not to use it for drawer boxes. All the parts must be the same thickness.

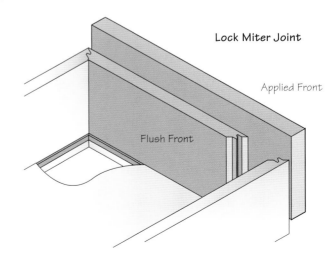

Lock Miter Joint

Applied Front

Flush Front

A final locking joint is the *lock miter*, which combines the appearance of a miter with the strength of a lock joint. The lock miter can be cut on the table saw, but it's more commonly cut with a special router bit or shaper knives. Only one set-up is needed. The first piece is run through standing on end against the fence, the second flat on the table. One hitch is that both parts have to be the same thickness.

The *sliding dovetail* is strong and easy to make (once you have the setup), but you can't cut the dovetail slot close by an edge. Thus, it will work only on an overlay drawer (or a flush drawer on commercial side-mounted slides). You can produce through and stopped joints; in the former, the dovetail slot is visible in the top edge of the drawer front, in the latter it is not.

A joint that looks akin to a dovetail is the *box joint*. It's strictly a machine-made joint (cut using a router or table saw), and it doesn't have as sophisticated an interlock as the dovetail. The many gluing surfaces make up for that and yield a joint that's plenty strong for drawers. You can even make half-blind forms of the box joint, though such aren't shown here. You can use the box joint in the same functional (but not aesthetic) applications you would the dovetail.

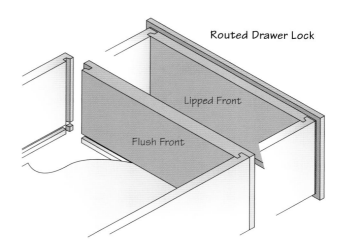

Routed Drawer Lock

Lipped Front

Flush Front

A specialty router bit (or shaper cutter) cuts both the drawer sides and its front to form this interlocking joint. The bit can also groove the drawer-box parts for a plywood bottom. One bit setting works for all cuts, though the fence must be shifted between cuts. Front and sides can be different thicknesses. Often used for plywood drawers getting applied fronts.

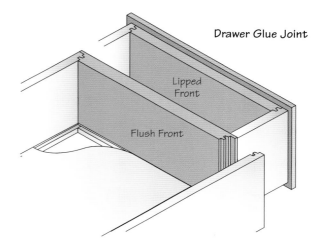

Drawer Glue Joint

Lipped Front

Flush Front

A seldom-seen variation of the routed drawer lock is the drawer glue joint. It's cut on the router table using a downsized glue-joint bit. The setup routine is slightly different, but the cutting sequence is the same. The cut profile has shoulders flanking the interlocking tongues, the better to resist wracking. Front and sides can be different thicknesses.

It's called a box joint because it was invented as a woodworking industrial joint to construct wooden boxes for packaging and shipping. Cut the slots on a table saw or router table. The process is tedious, but creates lots of long-grain to long-grain glue surface, yielding a strong joint. Unless the exposed joinery is part of the design, use an applied front.

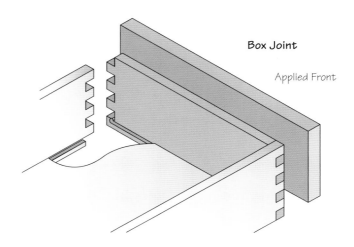

Box Joint

Applied Front

Dovetails generally indicate a well-made drawer. Through dovetails aren't universally acceptable for front-to-side joinery. They are strong but they show to the front as well as the side. If exposed joinery is part of the design, then that's okay. Otherwise, a false front is needed to conceal them.

The half-blind dovetail is the traditional joint for this application. It has been the joint of choice for literally centuries. Two hundred years ago, when glues were iffy and nails were dear, the hand-cut dovetail was just about the only joinery option for drawers. It was used on low-end furniture as well as high. Now that there are strong glues available and machine-cut joint options, half-blind dovetails are primarily on high-end and custom-made drawers.

The half-blind dovetail doesn't show to the front, but when the drawer is opened, it makes a great impression.

If half-blind dovetails have drawbacks, they stem from the effort it takes to make the joint. They are time-consuming to cut by hand and finicky to fit. You can use a router and one of several jigs to machine them, but dialing in the proper settings of jig and router can take time. And even with the most adjustable of the jigs, the results are pretty clearly machine-cut.

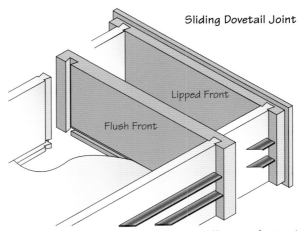

Sliding Dovetail Joint

Lipped Front

Flush Front

Use manufactured slides

The sliding dovetail is a routed joint that provides a strong connection between sides and front, provided you locate it properly. Overhang is essential at the ends of the drawer front, so it's a good joint to use for drawers with mechanical slides. The front can be configured as flush, lipped or overlay.

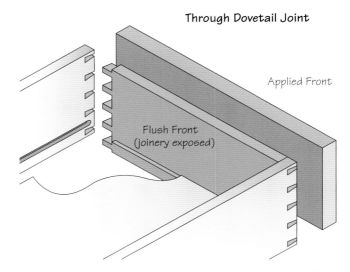

Through Dovetail Joint

Applied Front

Flush Front
(joinery exposed)

Through dovetails are not universally acceptable for front-to-side joinery. If exposed joinery is part of the design, then they're okay because they show to the front as well as the sides. Otherwise, an applied front is needed to conceal them. Through dovetails are easier to hand-cut than half-blinds. And many jigs are available to assist in routing them.

The half-blind dovetail is *the* traditional joint for joining the front and sides of a drawer. It can be used with either flush or lipped fronts, and it joins materials of different thicknesses. Most routed forms of the joint have uniform-size pins and tails, while hand-cutting allows tiny pins and wide tails. It's attractive, and you get a great mechanical connection to boot.

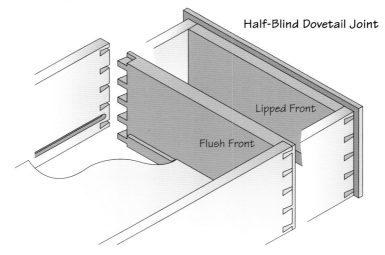

Half-Blind Dovetail Joint

Lipped Front

Flush Front

Side-to-Back Joinery

Function is more significant in the side-to-back joinery than appearance. It's common to find one joint used at the front and a different one at the back. The illustrations show some options.

Historically, through dovetails were used at the back of a drawer. In custom work, they are still the joint of choice.

When making the front joints with a particular machine set-up, make the back joints the same way.

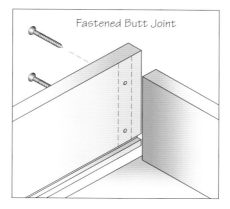
Fastened Butt Joint

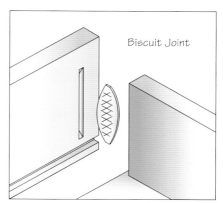
Biscuit Joint

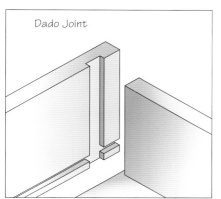
Dado Joint

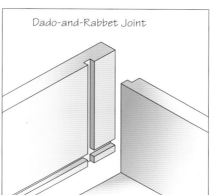
Dado-and-Rabbet Joint

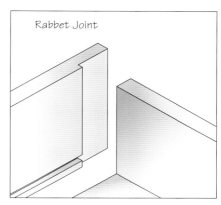
Rabbet Joint

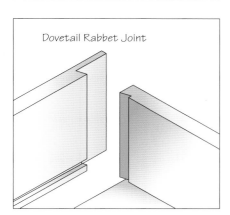
Dovetail Rabbet Joint

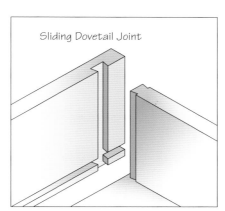
Sliding Dovetail Joint

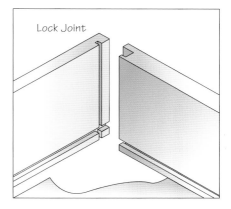
Lock Joint

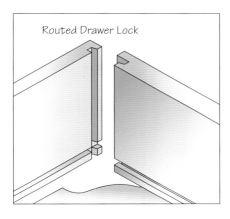
Routed Drawer Lock

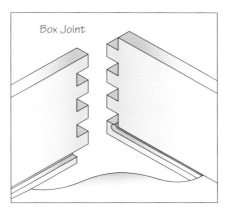
Box Joint

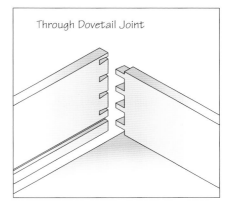
Through Dovetail Joint

Bottom Constructions

The bottom keeps the drawer's contents from falling on through. So the bottom has to be strong enough to support whatever you put in the drawer. But the joinery between the bottom and the walls of the drawer must also be strong.

The first issue to settle is the joinery. With few exceptions, drawer bottoms are housed in grooves cut in the drawer's front and sides. Sometimes in the back as well. Just bear in mind that the groove compromises the strength of the side at the most critical location. A groove that's too wide or too deep carries — along with the bottom — the potential for failing. And a thin side simply sharpens the dilemma.

A traditional solution to the problem is the drawer slip. Drawer slips are square strips of wood glued to the inner faces of the sides. The grooves for the bottom are cut in the slips. Therefore, a reasonably-sized groove isn't going to compromise the material.

Slips have an additional benefit. Thin sides that slide on runners gradually wear down over the years, detracting from a good fit. Drawer slips increase the bearing surface and thereby extend the probable life of the drawer.

On the other hand, slips are extra parts to be crafted and installed. (If you are doing woodworking as a business, you won't be designing slips into drawers. If you're an amateur, you need to make the occasional piece with slips in its drawers.)

Choose a material next. Will the bottom be solid wood or plywood? As noted previously, plywood tends to be the choice for all but the traditional chest of drawers. At any given thickness, it is as strong as solid wood. It is stable, so movement isn't a problem. In fact, it can be glued in place, which helps stiffen the box. And the economics of it are excellent.

We tend to use birch or maple plywood for drawer bottoms without much thought involved. But keep in mind that 1/4" plywood faced in a variety of other species is available from plywood dealers — not home centers but plywood dealers.

The primary drawback to plywood is the actual thickness. A 1/4" sheet is really about 7/32", and even that is an average across the sheet. If you cut a 1/4" groove for the stuff, it'll rattle. The solution is to use a less-than-1/4" cutter, and make two passes to match the groove width to the sheet thickness.

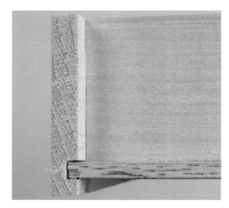

Relatively few drawers are made with bottoms other than 1/4" plywood. It is lightweight and strong, inexpensive and easy to work with.

If you believe the application requires a thicker, stronger bottom — 1/2" plywood used here — don't fail to bulk up the drawer sides and the groove for the bottom as well.

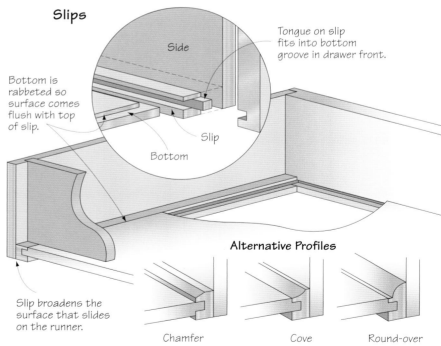

Slips

Side

Tongue on slip fits into bottom groove in drawer front.

Bottom is rabbeted so surface comes flush with top of slip.

Slip

Bottom

Slip broadens the surface that slides on the runner.

Alternative Profiles

Chamfer   Cove   Round-over

Solid-Wood Bottoms

The alternative is the traditional solid-wood bottom. Unless the bottom is very small, it needs to be thicker than $1/4$" (thin wood being prone to crack). A typical solid-wood bottom thickness is $1/2$", though smaller drawers might have $3/8$" bottoms. Some furniture makers favor $5/8$" bottoms.

To reduce the width of the groove required, the edges of such a bottom will get a tongue or a rabbet, or it will be raised. You can use a panel-raising bit in a table-mounted router to mill the bottoms, and you will get a nicely formed tongue to fit the grooves.

A solid bottom should be used only in open-back construction. You must orient the grain side to side, parallel to the back. These measures direct expansion out the back. To ensure that the bottom can expand and contract, use a screw (or a nail) in a slotted hole to secure it to the drawer back.

On a very wide drawer a large, one-piece bottom is likely to sag, and it may eventually break. You can deal with this before it becomes a problem by adding a center muntin. This frame piece, which extends from front to back, divides the bottom opening of the drawer box so two smaller panels can be used to form the bottom. The muntin must be grooved like the sides, and it must be securely anchored to the front and back. You can use a tongue or dovetail at the front, while a rabbet cut across the muntin at the back to form a simple lap joint between it and the drawer back.

Two small drawer-bottom panels are stronger than one large one. A muntin divides the drawer box's bottom (just the way it divides a window) so two panels can be used instead of one.

Muntin

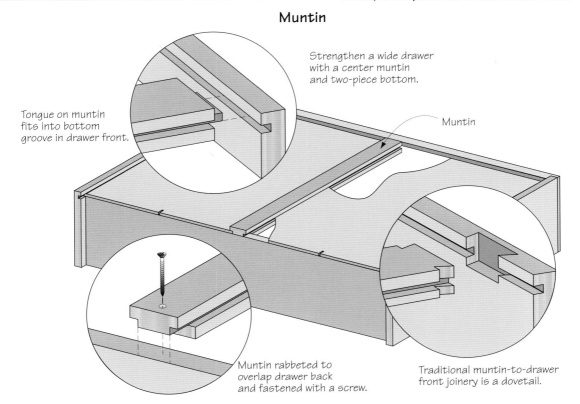

Strengthen a wide drawer with a center muntin and two-piece bottom.

Tongue on muntin fits into bottom groove in drawer front.

Muntin

Muntin rabbeted to overlap drawer back and fastened with a screw.

Traditional muntin-to-drawer front joinery is a dovetail.

CHAPTER TWO

Supporting a Drawer

A drawer alone — just an open box — is an oddity. For it to work as intended, it has to be installed in a case in a way that allows it to be opened and closed. The movement has to be smooth, and once open, the drawer has to be able to stay open without your help. This movement can be controlled in several ways. Some mounting systems are integral to the case, while others are add-ons. Regardless, the mounting system should be carefully planned along with the case and drawer design.

Runners, Guides, and Kickers

Most of the subassemblies that support drawers in a case or table must be incorporated as you build the piece itself. Sure, hardware makes it easy, though fairly expensive, to hang drawers in an open, undifferentiated case, but this approach is largely limited to kitchen cabinetry and similar built-ins. Most of what we consider "furniture" is built using traditional approaches.

The traditional approach to casework is to partition the case using drawer dividers. A divider is a rail — and, yes, a lot of woodworkers just call it a rail — extending from one side of the case to the other. It separates the drawers visually and physically.

But drawer dividers do more than separate one drawer pocket from another. They also keep the case sides straight and parallel. As such, they need to be integral to the overall design and construction of the case.

ABOVE   A chest of drawers may use the case bottom as the support for the lowest drawer and simple frames composed of dividers and runners to support the others. The solid chest walls guide each drawer into its pocket.

TOP LEFT   In cabinetry constructed from sheet goods, the interior is sometimes divvied up into drawer pockets with solid panels. It's an expedient approach, since you neither have to dress stock for dividers and runners nor cut joinery to assemble frames.

BOTTOM LEFT   If drawers of different widths are to be housed in a chest, the internal architecture is bound to be more complicated. In the lower portion of this chest (viewed from the back), full-width drawers are supported by dividers and runners that are attached to the case sides. The top two tiers house multiple drawers, so back rails are used to support intermediate runners and guides.

A stopped dado is a simple way to join a drawer divider to the case side. Rout a shallow dado, just a bit shorter than the divider's width, and square the ends with a chisel. Notch the front corner of the divider. Fitted snugly and glued, the joint is sound.

In a case for lipped drawers, a shouldered half-blind dovetail looks better because it shifts the tail out from under the lip, so it can be seen. Cut a dado, then rout the dovetail slot.

A half-blind dovetail, often called a sliding dovetail in this application, joins divider and case side in a way that resists tension stresses well (even without glue). The tail on the divider's end slides into a matching slot in the case side. Just one divider holds the case sides in place, making case assembly fairly easy for the lone woodworker. Two or three raps with a dead blow mallet will seat a properly fitted joint.

Installing Runners

Of course you need more than a drawer divider to support a drawer — you need runners under each drawer side. A runner, simply, is a strip of wood that extends from the divider to the back of the case. Typically, the runner is joined to the divider with some form of tenon — either a conventional mortise and tenon or a stub tenon housed in a groove.

Inevitably in casework, the runner is cross-grain to the side. It's got to be attached to the side, of course, but in a way that allows the side to expand and contract. Otherwise, it can prompt the side to split or buckle.

TOP RIGHT   The mortise-and-tenon is the traditional way of joining runners to the drawer dividers. Assemble the joint without glue so the tenon can shift in and out in the mortise. Though the case side to which the runner is fastened expands and contracts, the runner stays connected to the divider.

MIDDLE RIGHT   A loose tenon fitted to matching mortises in the runner and divider is a modern variation of the mortise and tenon.

BOTTOM RIGHT   A quick-and-easy connection between runner and divider is afforded by the groove and stub tenon. You cut the groove — stopped or through — with a slot cutter on the router table. Then lower the cutter slightly and cut the stubby tenons with it.

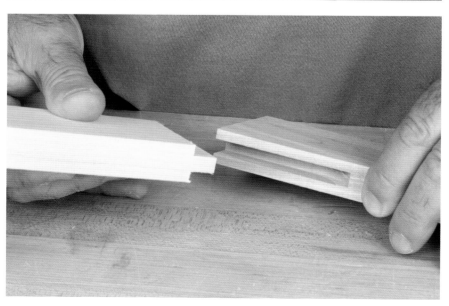

LEFT Runners can be seated in a shallow dado cut across the case side. Use no glue in the assembly. A tenon — a loose one here — joins the runner to the divider, and screws driven through oversized or elongated holes in the runner fasten it to the case side. The dado aligns the runner and keeps it from sagging.

BELOW LEFT A simple method from the 17th and 18th centuries is to join the runner to the divider with an unglued mortise-and-tenon and nail the back end to the case side. When the side expands and contracts, the tenon shifts slightly in and out of the mortise.

BELOW In a case with full-width drawers, no back rail is necessary. Chamfer the end of the runner to reduce the length of mounting screw you need, and screw it to the case side. Building in a period of high humidity? Leave a gap of about 1/8" between the runner's shoulders and the divider's edge. The joint with the divider is unglued, and the gap will close as humidity declines.

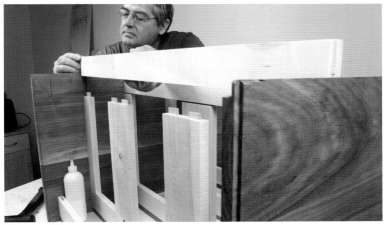

Where a runner will be trapped between the divider and a back rail, you can glue the mortise and tenon between the runner and the front rail (LEFT), leaving the joint with the back rail unglued. Join the runners to the divider, then set the rail in place and drive it home (ABOVE).

Web Frames

Often, the system of drawer dividers and runners is turned into a complete frame, with two (or more) runners trapped between rails front and back. The resulting frame, usually called a web frame, can be constructed and installed in a variety of ways, all derivative of how drawer dividers and runners are joined to each other and to case sides.

The drawing (bottom) shows a workable way of constructing and installing a web frame. Typically, the parts of the web frame are not glued together, though the frame rails are glued to the case.

In most cases, the runners should be slightly (about ⅛") short at the back so that the side can shrink, closing this gap between the runner and the back rail without pushing the rail out.

In a frame-and-panel (or post-and-panel) assembly, wood movement is moot. The runner can be edge-glued to a rail in the side assembly, or it can be set into dadoes in the side assembly stiles and glued, so long as it isn't glued to the panel. The runner could also be mortised into a drawer divider and glued to the back stile.

In plywood construction, a runner can be glued into a shallow dado or simply glued and screwed directly to the plywood side.

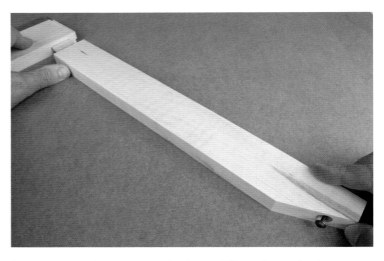

The simplest web frame consists of a drawer divider and a couple of runners. Here, the runner is linked to the divider with an unglued loose tenon. A single screw will fasten the back end to the case side, fixing the runner at that spot. As the case side expands and contracts, the space between the runner and divider will vary.

Typical Web Frame Construction

Properly assembled and mounted, a web frame allows solid-wood casework to expand and contract. Cut the runners about ⅛" short and join them to the drawer divider with glued mortise-and-tenons. Leave the joint between runners and back rail unglued to allow the case sides to move.

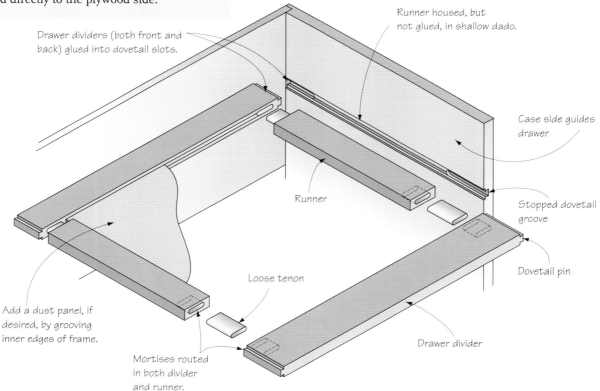

Drawer dividers (both front and back) glued into dovetail slots.

Runner housed, but not glued, in shallow dado.

Case side guides drawer

Runner

Stopped dovetail groove

Dovetail pin

Loose tenon

Add a dust panel, if desired, by grooving inner edges of frame.

Mortises routed in both divider and runner.

Drawer divider

Keep a drawer's contents clean by fitting a dust panel into a web frame. Before plywood was invented, a solid-wood panel would be incorporated to double as a runner. Nowadays, plywood or hardboard panels are fitted to the web frames.

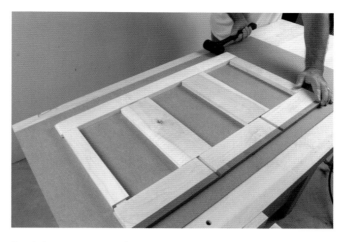

A web frame to support three drawers needs a back rail. All the runners are suspended between it and the drawer divider using loose tenons. The divider has two dovetail grooves for vertical dividers, and drawer guides will be glued to the wide runners.

Web Frame in a Post-and-Panel Case

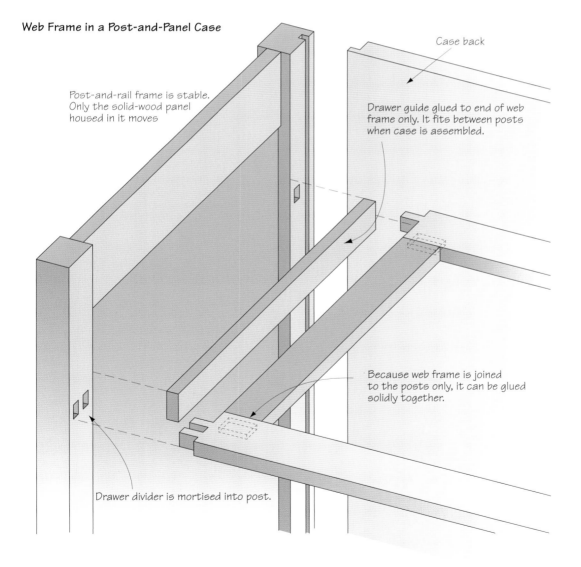

Post-and-rail frame is stable. Only the solid-wood panel housed in it moves

Case back

Drawer guide glued to end of web frame only. It fits between posts when case is assembled.

Because web frame is joined to the posts only, it can be glued solidly together.

Drawer divider is mortised into post.

Guides

A drawer's movement in and out of its "pocket" usually is directed by the case sides. But sometimes, as in a case with a face-frame or a post-and-panel case, you need drawer guides. The guides form a channel just a tad wider than the drawer (so the drawer can't get cocked and wedged half-closed).

Guides are sometimes needed to control the drawer as it moves in and out of its pocket. In this utilitarian cabinet with a face frame, extra strips of wood attached to the web frame form a channel just wide enough for the drawer.
1. Guides

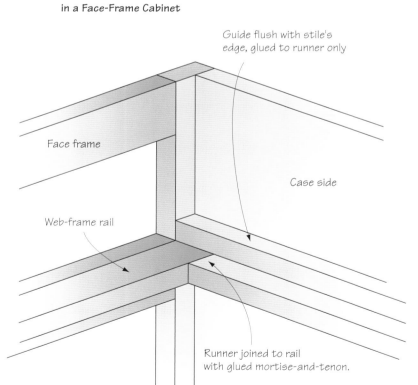

Runner and Guide
in a Face-Frame Cabinet

Guide flush with stile's
edge, glued to runner only

Face frame

Case side

Web-frame rail

Runner joined to rail
with glued mortise-and-tenon.

Chances are that a drawer in a frame-and-panel chest will cock slightly when you close it and the end of the side will jam against the side assembly's rear stile. So a guide, planed flush with the stiles, must be glued to the drawer runner, so the drawer always opens and closes smoothly without jamming.

Center Runners and Guides

Side-by-side drawers, often included in dressers and other chests, need support in the middle of the chest, away from the sides. The usual approach here is to suspend a wide runner between the drawer divider in front and a rail in back. A vertical divider with a guide behind it separates the neighboring drawers.

Two wide runners and two narrow runners trapped between a drawer divider and a back rail form a web frame to support three drawers. This is a test fitting. As I assemble the case, I'll glue the divider to the case sides, then the runners to the divider, and finally glue the back rail to the case but not to the runners.

Vertical drawer dividers partition the low, wide space between horizontal dividers into narrower drawer pockets. This divider is joined to the assembly with sliding dovetails.

To control the movement of the drawers, glue guides to the wide runners, directly behind the vertical drawer dividers. A wide straight scrap, set against the vertical divider and clamped to the horizontal divider, aligns the guide.

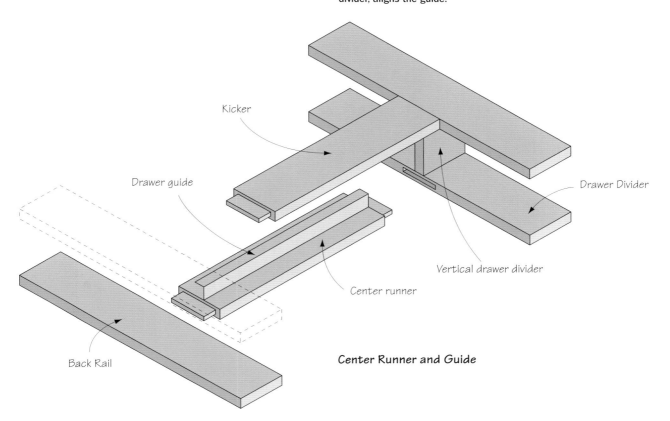

Kicker

Drawer guide

Drawer Divider

Vertical drawer divider

Center runner

Back Rail

Center Runner and Guide

Kickers

An important element in most drawer mounting systems is the kicker. A kicker prevents the drawer from tipping down as it is pulled open. It is just like a runner, but generally, it's mounted above the drawer side. A single center kicker may be used for a top drawer.

Stationed just above a drawer, the kicker keeps it level as it's pulled open. Typically in a chest of drawers, a runner doubles as the kicker for the drawer beneath it. That's the case in this chest, despite the staggered arrangement of its drawers.

Side Kicker

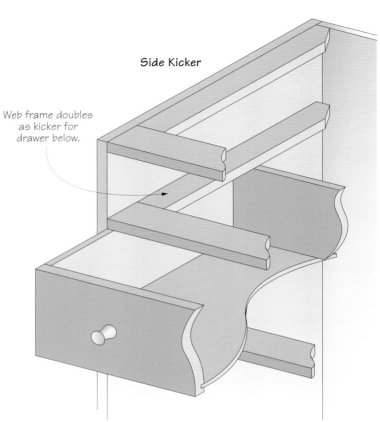

Web frame doubles as kicker for drawer below.

Center Kicker

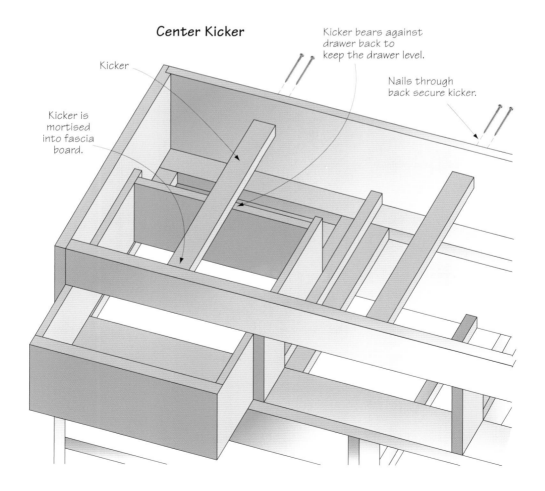

Kicker

Kicker is mortised into fascia board.

Kicker bears against drawer back to keep the drawer level.

Nails through back secure kicker.

Runner, Guide and Kicker in a Table

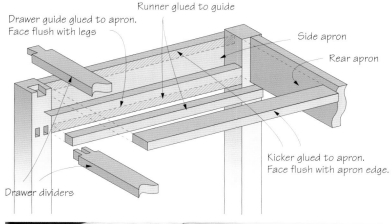

Drawer guide glued to apron. Face flush with legs

Runner glued to guide

Side apron

Rear apron

Kicker glued to apron. Face flush with apron edge.

Drawer dividers

Sturdy framing supports multiple drawers in a table. A vertical divider mortised into upper and lower rails stiffens them. The runner and kicker, also mortised into the rails, double as cross members. The drawer guide is glued to the runner.

At the back, the runner and kicker are mortised into the apron.

Tables with Drawers

Adding a drawer or two to a table makes it more useful. A drawer in a bedside table holds (and hides) what would otherwise clutter the tabletop. In the kitchen, it becomes a work table, the drawer holding utensils. In the den, drawers in a table transform it into a desk.

But drawers make engineering the table more challenging because it occupies space where a solid apron would otherwise be. A critical design variable is the drawer's width. If the drawer (or drawers) span the space from leg to leg, then a double rail construction is appropriate. Two rails, turned on edge, connect the legs, forming a drawer pocket. The top rail is almost always let into the top of the legs with a dovetail joint. The bottom rail joins the legs with either a twin mortise-and-tenon joint or a sliding dovetail.

The same sorts of runners and guides and kickers that support drawers in a case serve in the table. But because the table's aprons almost invariably have their grain running from leg to leg, you can just glue the parts in place. You don't have to accommodate wood movement.

Two drawers fitted side-by-side under a table top are always separated by a vertical divider, and it ought to join the horizontal drawer rails with either a twin mortise-and-tenon or a sliding dovetail joint. The latter offers the best structural support because it locks the parts together mechanically in a way the other two joints do not.

Behind the vertical divider, of course, must be a center runner, guide and kicker almost exactly like what you'd use in a case. Instead of back rails, you'd mortise the runner and kicker into the back apron, or better, into ledgers glued to, and stiffening, the apron.

A couple of cautions are in order. When planning a table with drawers, remember that the wider the span, the more likely it is that the drawer-rail assembly will sag. Remember too that the total height of the drawer rail assembly should be no more than 6" if you expect to sit with your legs under the table.

Side-Mounted Runners

Mounting the runners beside the drawer rather than under it changes a number of things. It eliminates some substantial parts that, though they do stiffen and reinforce the case, take time to make and assemble. Without drawer dividers, the case is opened up allowing you to stretch the height of your drawers.

The concept is simple and so is the construction. The runners are relatively slender, roughly 3/8" by 1", strips of a hard and stable stock that you fasten to the case sides. Grooves cut in the drawer's sides mate with the runners. Not only do the runners support the drawer as it is opened and closed, they double as kickers and drawer stops.

A face frame cabinet can be outfitted with side-hung drawers, as can a table. A piece's style shouldn't obviate the use of side-hung drawers.

Several caveats apply. First, the bay for the drawer or drawers must be straight and square. The runners must be attached to a solid-wood case side in a way that allows the side to expand and contract. Screws in slots rather than tight pilots work in this regard. In addition, the drawer sides must be thick enough to accommodate the groove; you should leave a minimum of a 1/4" of stock between the groove bottom and the inside of the drawer.

Take those cautions to heart as you design your project and you'll find that installing side-hung drawers is straight-forward, producing perfectly fitted, smooth-gliding drawers in a chest or table that is not beyond your abilities.

Side-Hung Drawers

Wooden runners attached to case sides mate with grooves in the drawer sides. The runners support the drawer in open and closed positions and double as kickers and closing stops.

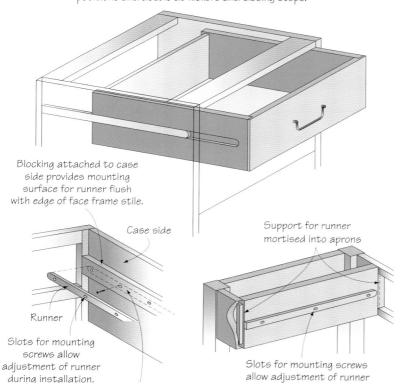

Blocking attached to case side provides mounting surface for runner flush with edge of face frame stile.

Case side

Support for runner mortised into aprons

Runner

Slots for mounting screws allow adjustment of runner during installation.

Slots for mounting screws allow adjustment of runner during installation.

Blocking is screwed, not glued, to solid-wood side; slots for screws allow side to expand and contract.

Face Frame Casework

Leg-and-Apron Construction

Some furniture designs, such as this case without dividers separating the drawers, make it difficult to use conventional runners. Use side-mounted slides instead. The slides are just strips of wood attached to the case sides that mate with grooves cut in the drawer sides.

Grooving the Drawers

Side-mounted runners are made and mounted in a case only after the drawers have been assembled. And the runners are made to fit grooves cut in the drawer sides. So cutting the grooves is where we begin.

While you can certainly cut grooves in the drawer sides before assembling the drawers, you'll achieve more accurate results if you wait until the drawer is glued up. Because the grooves are stopped, you must rout them rather than using the table saw. By simply setting the drawer's back about 1/4" below the sides, you'll be able to groove the drawers accurately and safely on the router table.

The trick is to fasten or clamp a stop to the fence, directly over the bit. The stop can only project about 1/4" beyond the fence's face. Because the drawer back is slightly recessed, it clears the stop as you feed the drawer across the bit, but the front hits the stop. The drawing shows how to establish the width of the stop.

Here's the setup for routing side-runner grooves in drawer sides. The stop is fastened to the fence, centered over the bit and projecting 1/8" to 1/4". The pencil lines help align the fence with the bit when adjusting it to accommodate different drawer sizes.

As you start the cut in the right side of a drawer (LEFT), the recessed back clears the stop and allows you to advance the drawer onto the bit. The drawer front isn't recessed, so it hits the stop and arrests the groove (ABOVE).

To groove the left side of the drawer, you begin with the front against the stop and the drawer tipped back so it is clear of the bit. Tip the drawer down onto the bit and advance it until it has moved beyond the bit.

Sizing and Placing Stop for Routing Runner Groove

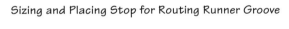
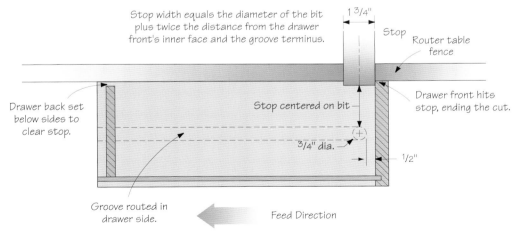

Stop width equals the diameter of the bit plus twice the distance from the drawer front's inner face and the groove terminus.

1 3/4"

Stop

Router table fence

Drawer front hits stop, ending the cut.

Stop centered on bit

Drawer back set below sides to clear stop.

3/4" dia.

1/2"

Groove routed in drawer side.

Feed Direction

Cutting Runner and Groove

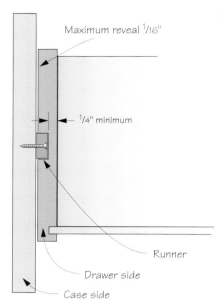

Maximum reveal ¹/₁₆"

¹/₄" minimum

Runner

Drawer side

Case side

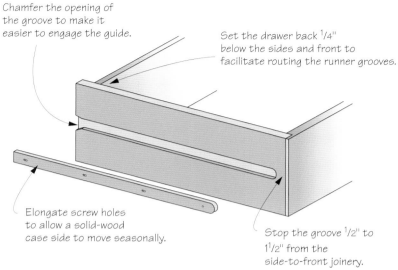

Chamfer the opening of the groove to make it easier to engage the guide.

Set the drawer back ¹/₄" below the sides and front to facilitate routing the runner grooves.

Elongate screw holes to allow a solid-wood case side to move seasonally.

Stop the groove ¹/₂" to 1¹/₂" from the side-to-front joinery.

LEFT Size the runners to fit the grooves in the drawers. The stock should be about ¹/₁₆" thicker than the groove depth and planed to slide smoothly with very little slop. Sand or file the nose to match the routed groove end.

BOTTOM LEFT Drill counter bores and shank holes for mounting screws. Those in the middle and back end of the runner should be elongated to allow adjustment of the runner during installation and to accommodate movement of the case side over the long haul.

BOTTOM RIGHT Make it a little easier to engage the drawer on the runner by slightly widening the end of the groove. Use a wide chisel and chamfer both edges of all the grooves.

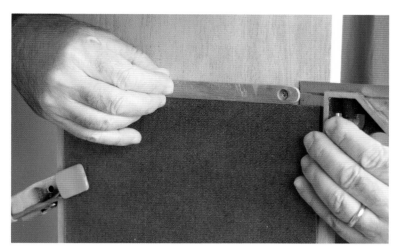

A Position Gauge Simplifies Installation

The key to perfect alignment of the pairs of runners is a piece of hardboard or plywood — something cheap. You cut it to match the height from the case bottom to the underside of the uppermost runners and about an 1" less than the case depth.

Clamp it to a case side, set a runner on top, and screw the runner to the case. Shift the gauge to the other side of the case and install the second runner. Once both are installed, cut down the gauge and install the next lower pair of runners.

To ensure that front-to-back alignment is accurate, mark the back edge of the spacer near the bottom and keep that edge oriented to the back for each pair of runners.

TOP LEFT With the gauge clamped to the case side, set a runner on top. To establish the set-back from the case front, use a square set to the distance from the drawer front to the groove. Apply a clamp to hold the runner.

LEFT Screw the runner to the case. Make it easy to fine-tune the fore-and-aft adjustment by driving only the screws in the slotted shank holes. After you've fitted all the drawers, you can go back and drive the last screws that fix each runner's position. Shift the gauge to the other side of the case and mount the second runner.

Fit each drawer as you go, making it right before cutting down the gauge. If the fit is too tight, plane or sand the runners to increase the clearance. Check how it relates to the drawer above. And check the reveal. If it isn't right, loosen the screws and slide the runners to the front or back as needed.

Once the uppermost drawer fits just right, cut down the gauge to install the next pair of runners. Screw them in place, fit the drawer and repeat the process until all the runners are in place and all the drawers fitted. Then drive those last screws to fix the runners.

Center-Mounted Runner and Slide

Wide drawers supported by side runners have a tendency to cock slightly as they are moved and that often causes them to bind. The wider the drawer, the more likely it is this will happen.

A single center-mounted runner and slide is the solution. The slide, which is attached to the underside of the drawer, has a channel in it that rides over a runner that's attached to the apron or web frame, as shown in the drawing. Installed correctly, a center-mount allows you to open and close a drawer from either corner, no binding.

It works with flush or lipped drawers, even with overlay drawers. As a bonus, the runner doubles as a closing stop.

In addition to working well with wide drawers, the system is great wherever the case sides can't guide the drawer, for example, with irregularly shaped drawers or ordinary drawers in irregularly shaped casework. If the drawer is small, you can use the center runner and slide to support the drawer as well as guide it, thus eliminating runners under the drawer sides.

According to the late Tage Frid, well-known furniture-maker, teacher and author, the center runner and slide is a reasonable fix for a slightly out-of-square drawer that can't be trued or a slightly undersized drawer that racks and binds in its pocket. But he did add that he'd use the method only as a last resort, because he regarded it as a lot of trouble to execute.

So there it is: the system has a reputation for being difficult. As a guy sometimes tarnished with that tag, I commiserate. And I say it's not true. Yes, it requires extra material and extra steps, but difficult it is not. There are no shortcuts to anywhere worth going.

Wide drawers are notorious for cocking and jamming, particularly when pulled or pushed by one knob alone. A center-mounted slide prevents sticking.

Center-Mounted Runner and Slide

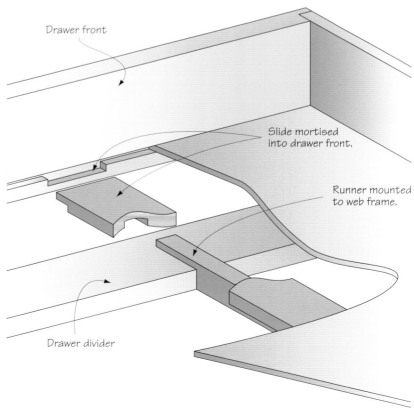

Drawer front

Slide mortised into drawer front.

Runner mounted to web frame.

Drawer divider

The most secure way to mount the runner to the web frame is in dadoes. Assemble the frame (with or without glue) and clamp a straightedge across it to guide your router. Cut a through dado across the back rail, a stopped dado in the drawer divider.

Use the same bit that cut the runner dadoes in the web frames to cut a groove in the slide that will be mounted underneath the drawer. A pass over the bit will yield a snug fit of the slide on the runner.

You need the slide to move without binding, but also without slop. Check the fit of the slide on the runner. The groove probably will need to be widened just a few thousands of an inch. Micro-adjust the router-table fence position, run the slide over the bit, recheck the fit. Repeat as necessary until you have the right fit.

Making the Runner and Slide

Though not essential, it's good practice to make both the runner and guide from quarter-sawn stock. Such stock minimizes the impact of seasonal wood movement on the guide system.

For the most robust construction, cut shallow dadoes across the front and back rails of the web frame before the case is assembled. With the runner locked in the dadoes, it can't be dislodged — not easily, anyway. Slightly easier is to glue and screw the guide to the web frame. Use a piece of hardboard as a spacer to place the guides consistently.

Here's a couple ways to join the slide to the drawer. One is to cut a stub tenon on the end of the slide and plug it into a mortise cut in the drawer front, right next to the groove for the bottom. An alternative is to open the mortise into a notch. When the slide is correctly aligned, fire a couple of brads through it into the drawer front.

Use a scrap of the working stock to establish the appropriate setback for the nose of the runner in its role as closing stop for the drawer. Fit the runners to the web frames and fasten them before assembling the case.

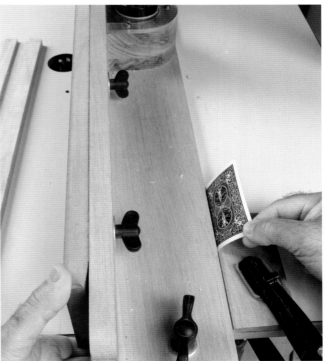

Widening the groove just the right amount can be tricky. Here's how to micro-adjust any router-table fence. Pinch a couple or three playing cards (each is consistently 0.010" thick) between the fence's back edge and a block clamped to the router-table top. Loosen the fence, remove the cards, and set the fence tight against the block. At the bit, you'll have moved the fence half the thickness of those cards.

Mount the Slide to the Drawer

The job of mounting the slide to the drawer begins after the case and drawers are assembled and the drawers are fitted to the case.

The nose of the guide is rabbeted, forming a barefaced tenon. You cut a mortise for it in the drawer front just below the groove for the drawer bottom. And the best way to locate the mortise is through a trial fitting.

1 Slide the drawer (without the bottom) into its pocket and gently butt it against the nose of the slide. Use playing cards to center the drawer by tucking an equal number of cards between the drawer and the case on either side.

2 ABOVE Wedge a slide on a runner in the case so the nose projects 3" to 6" beyond the edge of the drawer divider. A couple layers of masking tape over the runner should hold the slide.

3 Scribe around the nose of the guide on the inside of the drawer front.

4 Use a plunge router and edge guide to rout the mortise in the drawer front.

5 Check the fit of the slide's tenon in the mortise. You'll probably have to round off the tenon's corners with a chisel or file. Such paring can allow you to ease the slide left or right as you finalize the fit.

6 Slide the drawer bottom into its grooves, then mount the slide without gluing the tenon. Fit the drawer in the case, again using playing cards to center and wedge it in its pocket. Scribe along the edges of the slide on the drawer bottom.

7 With the drawer removed from the case, remove the slide. Apply a couple of patches of carpet tape to the drawer bottom between the pencil lines. Reinsert the slide's tenon in its mortise, align the slide carefully between the pencil lines and stick it to the drawer bottom.

8 Check the fit and action of the drawer in the case. If you are satisfied with it, pull the drawer out, drill pilot holes and screw the slide to the bottom and drawer back. A brad or two driven through the bottom edge of the drawer front will lock the slide's tenon.

Bottom Hung

A bottom-hung drawer is supported in the case by its bottom, which projects beyond the drawer sides and into channels in the case sides. The benefit is space efficiency. For every drawer you have, you gain at least an inch of vertical storage because the drawer itself doesn't extend below its bottom and because no runners are beneath the drawer.

I've seen old manufactured flat file drawers — used by architects, engineers, graphics folks, museums and others to store blueprints, posters, artwork — with dozens of large shallow drawers that used this construction. The bottom-hung construction allowed the maker to fit several extra drawers in any given case.

Cut a dado, extending from front to back, in each case side. The drawer bottom is wide enough to span from dado to dado. The drawer box sits atop the bottom, and the front overhangs the bottom on either side to conceal the dadoes when the drawer is closed.

Where the construction makes a lot of sense is in economical, functional storage pieces.

The edges of this bit drawer's ¼" plywood bottom project into grooves in the router table cabinet. The bottom hangs in those grooves and supports the drawer. Easy to make, practical to use.

Bottom-Mounted Drawer

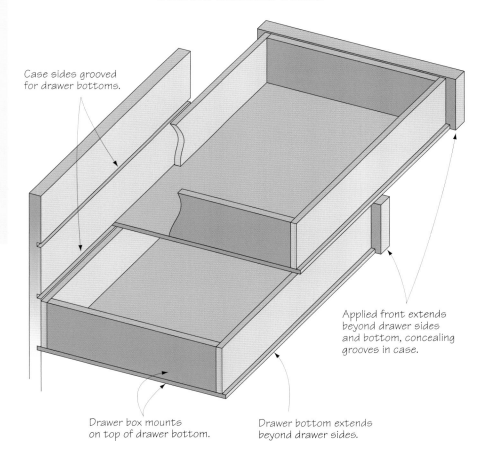

Case sides grooved for drawer bottoms.

Applied front extends beyond drawer sides and bottom, concealing grooves in case.

Drawer box mounts on top of drawer bottom.

Drawer bottom extends beyond drawer sides.

Top Mounts

The best example of the top-mounted drawer is a Shaker sewing table: An elegant round-topped pedestal table standing on arched tripod feet. And a box scabbed to the underside of the top. Clunk!

Top-mounted drawers always strike me as after-thoughts. You didn't design the piece — usually a table or bench — to have a drawer, so when you realized one was needed, you just couldn't integrate it into the design.

The commonplace construction is to glue and/or fasten slides to the drawer sides, right at the top. If the sides are thick enough and the expected load modest, you could groove the sides 1/2" or 3/4" below their top edges. Rabbet strips of wood to fit under the runners or into the grooves and attach them to the underside of the support surface, usually a tabletop.

Glue slides for top-mounting a drawer to the sides, flush with the top edges. This slide is 1/2" x 5/8" oak. To ensure a good bond to the pre-finished plywood side, I rabbeted the side and trimmed off the face veneer.

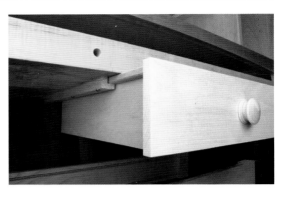

Mounted under my workbench, the drawer is a handy repository for frequently used tools. The applied front gussies up a "production drawer" (see page 155) and conceals the mounting.

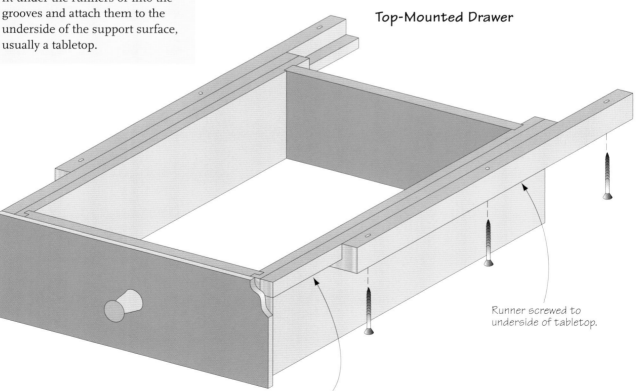

Top-Mounted Drawer

Runner screwed to underside of tabletop.

Cleat glued to drawer side.

Drawer Stops

Drawer stops keep all styles of drawers from falling out of their cases (opening stops) and flush drawers from sliding too far into their cases (closing stops).

A turn button is the simplest opening stop. It can be mounted on the inside of the drawer back or on the back edge of the front rail. Pivoting it out of the way allows the drawer to be inserted or removed.

A small block of wood tacked or glued to the back of the runner is the easiest way to make a closing stop. With the back removed and each drawer inserted so it's perfectly flush with the cabinet face, apply the closing stops with a dab of glue. Then add a couple brads or a small screw. You can also mount the closing stops onto the front rail, so they will catch against the back of the drawer front. They're definitely harder to locate and attach here, but such a stop could work for both opening and closing.

Keep a drawer from being opened too far and dumping its contents on the floor. A simple turn button screwed to the drawer back will stop the drawer when it contacts the drawer divider. To deliberately remove the drawer, twist the button a quarter turn.

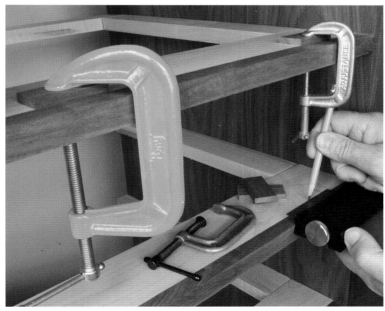

Mount stops — 3/16" x 1" x 3" pieces will do fine — on the drawer dividers to align the drawers uniformly and keep them from thumping the case back. Locate the stops — use two per drawer — by scribing a line on the divider with a marking gauge set to the drawer-front thickness.

An alternate location for closing stops is at the back of the drawer. By using a screw in a slot, you can adjust the stop's position slightly. But you do need access, so fit the drawers before installing the case back.

CHAPTER THREE

Choosing Materials

Though woodworkers are accustomed to making drawers from an assortment of materials, natural, solid wood is usually the first choice. It's the original choice, of course, so history and tradition favor it. The use of solid, natural wood throughout the drawer carries the marks of quality and craftsmanship.

The drawer front, of course, is made of the primary wood. But rarely do we make the rest of the drawer with that. Typically, we'll use a less spectacular, less costly wood for the sides and backs. Often, it's the same wood used for the seldom-seen parts in the casework. And the bottom is usually plywood.

To be honest, using solid wood for drawer boxes usually is more work, since you have to prep rough boards — and often resaw them in the bargain. Fitting solid-wood drawers to their case is trickier because wood expands and contracts seasonally.

Consequently, sheet goods are used almost exclusively for the drawer boxes in kitchen cabinetry and similar built-ins. The casework is uniform and modular, built of stable plywood and melamine-coated particleboard (MCP). The many drawers are supported on mechanical slides, which absorb most of the stresses that impact drawers. So the drawers themselves (excepting the show fronts) are made of plywood and assembled with simple joinery.

Choosing between solid wood and sheet goods is just the first step in selecting materials appropriate for your project's drawers. You should consider:

- Strength and weight
- Stability
- Wear-ability
- Appearance
- Cost

Weight and Strength

You want a drawer that is lightweight and strong. Strong enough to hold what you intend to put in the drawer, light enough that the drawer is easy to open and close. The trick is finding the balance between weight and strength. The drawer's support system enters into this calculation, as do aesthetics.

If the support system is a traditional wooden drawer sliding on wooden runners, both substantial strength and relatively light weight are important. If the drawer will be mounted on mechanical slides, the need for both is reduced. Mechanical slides generally make even the heaviest drawers easy to operate, thereby reducing stress on the drawer and thus reducing the strength required of the construction material.

Drawer proportions are the aesthetic component. We all have notions about proportions that are appropriate for drawers. One with sides too bulky for the drawer's overall dimensions gets your attention. So a wide, deep drawer in a dresser looks fine with sides as thick as $5/8$", but a smaller drawer in the same dresser looks out of proportion with sides that thick. The sides and back of a very small drawer — for a jewelry box or a traditional spice box, for example — need to be thin if the drawer is to look right.

How do you assess the strength of wood? Look up its specific gravity, which is the weight of a given volume of wood divided by the weight of the same volume of water. To wood technologists, specific gravity is a measure of wood density. The density of a wood is one of the best indicators of its strength. The higher the specific gravity, the denser — and stronger — the wood.

Wood technologists use several other measures of specific wood strengths, which are depicted in the wood strength chart. The data is taken from the *U.S. Forest Service's Wood Handbook*, which you can access (in .pdf format) online at www.fpl.fs.fed.us/.

Clockwise starting at upper left: Alder, poplar, soft maple and eastern white pine are among the most common secondary woods, dating back to the earliest dates of furniture-making in North America. All four are smooth, tight-grained woods of muted color that are easily worked.

WOOD STRENGTH

SPECIES	SPECIFIC GRAVITY	COMPRESSIVE STRENGTH	BENDING STRENGTH	STIFFNESS	HARDNESS
ALDER, RED	0.41	5820	9800	1.38	590
ASH	0.60	7410	15000	1.74	1320
BASSWOOD	0.37	4730	8700	1.46	410
BEECH	0.64	7300	14900	1.72	1300
BIRCH, YELLOW	0.62	8170	16600	2.01	1260
BUTTERNUT	0.38	5110	8100	1.18	490
CATALPA	0.41	N/A	N/A	1.21	550
CEDAR, EASTERN RED	0.47	6020	8800	0.88	900
CEDAR, WESTERN RED	0.34	3200	7700	1.11	350
FIR, DOUGLAS	0.48	7230	12400	1.95	710
HICKORY	0.72	9210	20200	2.16	N/A
MAPLE, HARD	0.63	7830	15800	1.83	1450
MAPLE, SOFT	0.54	6540	13400	1.64	950
OAK, RED	0.63	6760	14300	1.82	1290
OAK, WHITE	0.68	7440	15200	1.78	1360
PINE, EASTERN WHITE	0.35	4800	8600	1.24	380
PINE, SOUTHERN YELLOW	0.59	8470	14500	1.98	870
POPLAR, YELLOW	0.42	5540	10100	1.58	540
SASSAFRAS	0.46	4760	9000	1.12	630
SYCAMORE	0.49	5380	10000	1.42	770

Mounting a drawer on mechanical slides reduces the stresses to which it is subjected. It's the difference between sliding on ice and sliding on gravel. So the need for great strength in your drawer wood is lessened.

Wear-Ability

Wear-ability is a different measure. In a chest of traditional construction, the drawer rests on a frame composed of the drawer divider, runners and perhaps a back rail. The bottom edges of the sides are the bearing surfaces. Use a soft wood for the sides and/or the runners mounted in the chest, and the drawer will wear itself out of a good fit. The edges of the sides deteriorate, and perhaps grooves are worn in the runners (and even into the drawer divider).

It's worth mentioning too that in addition to wearing faster, soft woods slide more sluggishly.

The upshot here is that you want to use a reasonably durable wood as your secondary, and you want to use the same species for both the drawer sides and the runners.

LEFT The long-term durability of a piece of furniture depends in good part to the wear-ability of the species chosen as the secondary wood. After about a century of use, the drawers in this sideboard have worn grooves in the drawer dividers and runners.

BOTTOM To make long-wearing drawers, use hard woods like these. The two quarter-sawn oaks are particularly stable. Together with hickory, they display more vibrant figure than the maple, birch or ash.

1. Quarter-sawn White Oak
2. Birch
3. Quarter-sawn Red Oak
4. Ash
5. Hard Maple
6. Hickory

Stability

The traditional drawer opening, the one bounded by the case sides and the drawer dividers above and below, is in effect a frame that doesn't vary appreciably in dimension from season to season. A drawer made of solid wood does change appreciably in dimension from season to season. If too little overhead clearance is allowed, the drawer will stick in humid summers.

The upshot: Select your secondary wood based on its stability and the way it is sawed.

Woodworkers know that movement is primarily across a board's width rather than along its length; the length hardly changes at all. They also know boards are prone to cup, bow, twist, diamond and kink as their moisture content comes and goes. Many of these changes are a function of what part of the tree it came from and how it was sawn. (See the illustration How Wood Moves.)

But there's more. Different species of wood have different rates of shrinkage. Some, like mahogany (a favorite of cabinetmakers for centuries), teak, redwood, catalpa and northern white cedar, have reputations for stability; their dimensions change very little with humidity change. Others, like beech, certain oaks and hickory, change rather dramatically, and thus have reputations for being troublesome.

A good indicator of a wood's stability is its T/R ratio. Wood shrinks in three directions.

• The least movement occurs in the length of the board. An 8'-long board shrinks only about $^1/_{16}$" as it dries.

• The greatest movement is tangent to the growth rings, and it's called tangential movement. Looked at in terms of an entire long, the growth rings getting shorter in circumference. This movement is the "T" of the T/R ratio.

• Between these is movement perpendicular to the rings, which is called radial movement. As the log's growth rings shrink, the individual rings move closer together; the log's diameter declines. This movement is the "R" of the T/R ratio.

Naturally, radial movement is always less than tangential movement. But — and this is important — the relative difference between the two types of movement will vary widely among species. This is what the T/R ratio reflects.

As a general rule, the greater the difference between the tangential and radial values, the greater is the species' tendency to distort (twist, cup, warp, bow, etc.) during moisture content changes. It's trickier to dry in the first place, which is a challenge for the kiln operator. For the woodworker — presumably you — the risk is that it will distort when you dress the kiln-dried (but still rough-sawn) board, or subsequently during seasonal expansion and contraction.

Wood expands and contracts in three planes. It moves very little longitudinally (parallel to the grain), less than 0.1 percent of its length when originally cut. The significant movement is radial (perpendicular to the annual rings) and tangential (tangent to the annual rings). Radial movement averages 4 percent of the dimension when originally cut. Tangential movement averages 8 percent.

1. Tangential
2. Radial
3. Longitudinal

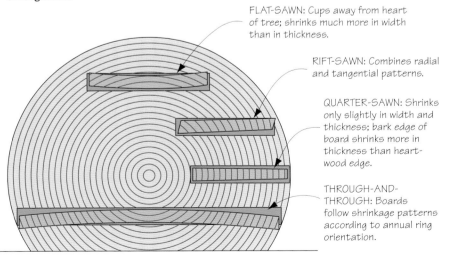

FLAT-SAWN: Cups away from heart of tree; shrinks much more in width than in thickness.

RIFT-SAWN: Combines radial and tangential patterns.

QUARTER-SAWN: Shrinks only slightly in width and thickness; bark edge of board shrinks more in thickness than heart-wood edge.

THROUGH-AND-THROUGH: Boards follow shrinkage patterns according to annual ring orientation.

How Wood Moves

Species Shrinkage

SPECIES	RADIAL	TANGENTIAL	T/R RATIO
ALDER, RED	4.4	7.3	1.7
ASH, WHITE	5.0	7.8	1.6
BASSWOOD	6.6	9.3	1.4
BEECH	5.5	11.9	2.2
BIRCH	7.3	9.5	1.3
BUTTERNUT	3.4	6.4	1.9
CATALPA	2.5	4.9	2.0
CEDAR, EASTERN RED	3.1	4.7	1.5
CEDAR, WESTERN RED	2.4	5.0	2.1
FIR, DOUGLAS	4.5	7.3	1.6
HICKORY, TRUE	7.0	10.5	1.5
MAPLE, HARD	4.8	9.9	2.1
MAPLE, SOFT	3.5	7.7	2.2
OAK, RED	4.0	8.6	2.2
OAK, WHITE	5.6	10.5	1.9
PINE, EASTERN WHITE	2.1	6.1	2.9
PINE, SOUTHERN YELLOW	4.7	7.3	1.6
POPLAR, YELLOW	4.6	8.2	1.8
SASSAFRAS	4.0	6.2	1.6
SYCAMORE	5.0	8.4	1.7

Sawing a Log

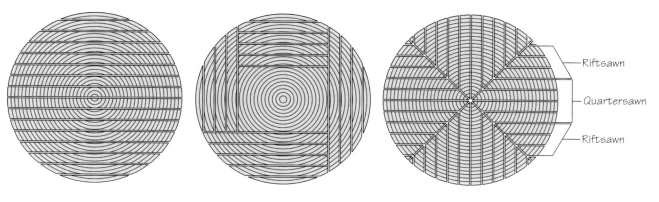

Sawed Through-and-Through   Sawed Around   Quartersawn

Because of the difference between tangential movement and radial movement, the orientation of the growth rings in a board determines how it will react as moisture content changes. So the way the board is cut from the log is important.

You probably know there are two broadly defined ways of cutting a log: plain-sawing and quarter-sawing.

A log can be plain-sawed in either of two ways. The simpler method is often called "sawing through-and-through." As suggested by the drawing, Sawing a Log, page 54, the blade cuts through the log again and again, creating boards the width of the log. Because the log stays in one position as it's cut up, the process is efficient and produces little waste.

A second plain-sawing method is called "sawing around." The log is slabbed until defects are encountered. Then it's rotated 90° and the cutting resumes. When defects are exposed, the log is rotated yet again. The end result is a pile of boards and a thick timber, often a square, containing the pith.

Quarter-sawing is more involved. Sawyers have a variety of routines, but in the main, the log is first cut into quarters. Each quarter then is sawed individually into boards. It's time-consuming and labor-intensive, and as a consequence, quarter-sawn lumber is more costly than plain-sawn.

There are advantages and disadvantages to both types of cutting, but when it comes to wood movement and distortion, quartersawn lumber will always distort less and move the least across its width as moisture content changes. Unfortunately, most lumber sold is flat-sawn. But as the drawing How Wood Moves, page 53, shows, it is quite possible to have a combination of quarter-sawn and flat-sawn grain in any one board.

Look at a board's end grain to determine how it's been cut. Growth rings oriented perpendicular to the faces reveal the top board to be quarter-sawn. In contrast, the general edge-to-edge orientation of the bottom board's rings reveal it to be plain-sawn. In between is a rift-sawn board, with rings oriented between 30° and 45° to the faces.

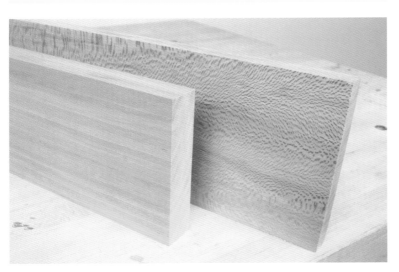

ABOVE In some species, the difference in figure between rift-sawn and quarter-sawn boards can be startling. Both boards are sycamore.

RIGHT Red oak is a favorite of many woodworkers. To my eye, anyway, the quarter-sawn (right) is better looking than the plain-sawn (left). Moreover, the quarter-sawn is more stable, a quality we want in drawers.

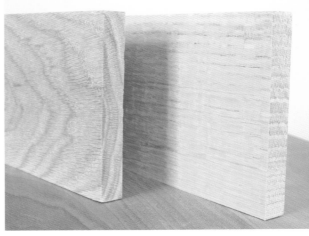

Attractiveness

A drawer is usually closed, right? The drawer boxes are a practical feature of even an elegant or eye-popping piece of furniture. No one, except the owner, sees the inside of the drawer. So why waste time and money on anything but an economical, proven secondary wood?

Bland thus becomes the default choice for a drawer wood.

Don't sell yourself and your work so short. A thoughtfully chosen drawer wood can subtly distinguish your chest of drawers, desk, sideboard or cupboard. Choose a species that pleasantly surprises when a drawer is opened. Perhaps it's an unexpected figure in the drawer wood that does it. Or a sharp color contrast between the drawer wood and the primary wood. Or a complementary color and texture.

Study the species you've chosen as the primary wood, and weigh its appearance against potential drawer woods. Look for good pairings of color, brightness and texture to give you the effect — complement or contrast — that you want.

Drawers need not be dowdy. Several species exhibit snappy flecks and rays when quartersawn. That visual appeal, coupled with better stability, makes their extra cost a good investment.
1. Quartersawn Red Oak
2. Quartersawn Sycamore
3. Quartersawn Beech
4. Butternut

When a drawer is closed, odors are trapped inside. Don't view this as a problem; it's an opportunity. Some species of wood have appealing scents. What could be better than a drawer made of aromatic cedar for your sweaters?
1. Western Red Cedar
2. Eastern Red Cedar
3. Sassafras

Matchmaking

Too often, the selection of a secondary wood is given little if any thought. "I use poplar" or "maple's always good" are two common responses to any query about woods to use for drawers.

But if you are planning a special chest or cupboard, one you're going to give your best woodworking effort, do some research and contemplate a departure from the wood you always use as a secondary. Here are four common primary woods — walnut, cherry, maple, and African mahogany. Each is matched with several suitable secondary woods.

But don't just take one of my suggestions. Put together your own collection of wood samples to help you make such choices, every time you tackle a new project.

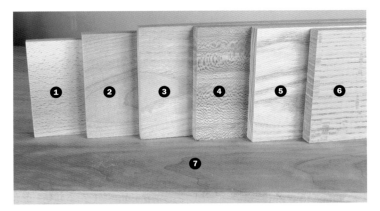

1. Quarter-sawn Beech
2. Birch
3. Sassafras
4. Quarter-sawn Sycamore
5. Ash
6. Quarter-sawn Red Oak
7. Cherry

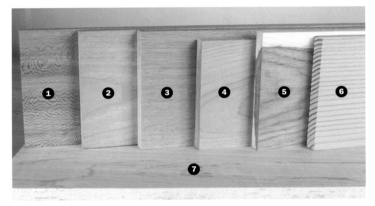

1. Quarter-sawn Sycamore
2. Sassafras
3. Quarter-sawn White Oak
4. Alder
5. Hickory
6. Douglas Fir
7. Maple

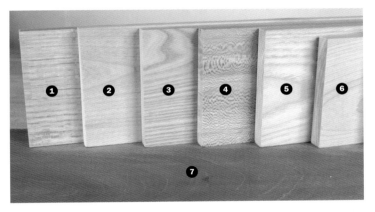

1. Quarter-sawn Red Oak
2. Alder
3. Catalpa
4. Quarter-sawn Sycamore
5. Sassafras
6. Birch
7. Mahogany

1. Birch
2. Maple
3. Ash
4. Poplar
5. Butternut
6. Walnut

Red Alder

White Ash

Basswood

Quartersawn Beech

American Birch

Butternut

Catalpa

Eastern Red Cedar

Western Red Cedar

Douglas Fir

Hickory

Hard Red Maple

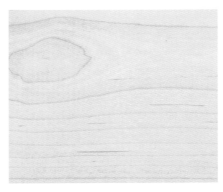

Soft Maple

Quartersawn Red Oak

Quartersawn White Oak

Eastern White Pine

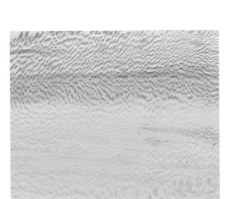

Southern Yellow Pine

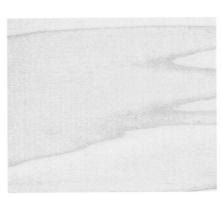

Yellow Poplar

Sassafras

Quartersawn Sycamore

Cost

Cost is the main rationale behind the use of a secondary wood. Poplar for the chests I built for the photographs cost only 20 or 25 percent of what I spent for cherry, walnut and hard maple.

But the material expense is only part of your cost calculation. Here I'm thinking primarily about drawer bottoms. I pointed out that in just minutes, you can produce a stack of drawer bottoms from a sheet of plywood. How long will it take to make a matching stack of solid-wood drawer bottoms?

That job usually entails resawing as well as the usual materials prep labor. Glue-ups typically are necessary to get panels 15" to 18" wide, which a drawer for a chest of drawers requires. Joinery cuts will be required in the bottom itself, either a rabbet or some sort of panel-raising operation.

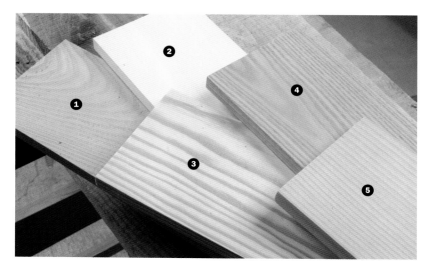

Look at all the species available at the sawmill or lumber dealer when selecting stock for drawers. Some economical, durable woods may be in the rack, just beyond the soft maple and poplar. Here are five examples:
1. Sassafras
2. Basswood
3. Southern Yellow Pine
4. Catalpa
5. Douglas Fir

LEFT Often, low-grade traditional cabinet woods are used for secondary purposes. Knots, splits, stains and discolorations all degrade a board, leading to a lower grade and thus a lower price per board-foot. But in a secondary application, many of those defects are immaterial.

Resawing

The sides, backs and bottoms of drawers typically are thinner than the fronts, so building drawers often requires 1/2" stock, 3/8" stock, even 1/4" stock for small drawers.

You can plane down 4/4 stock to these thicknesses. But if that entails removing much more than 1/8", you're wasting a lot of wood. It's far more economical to re-saw stock.

Out-of-the-ordinary machinery is not required. A conventional 14" band saw or 10" table saw can resaw stock up to 6" wide. I'd call that adequate for drawer stock; if wider boards are needed for deep drawers, make it by edge-gluing narrower boards, just as you would for a case side or tabletop.

Stock Preparation
Resawing creates a whole new surface, exposing the interior of the wood to the air. The upshot is this: Newly resawn boards usually warp and you must allow for it. Before your resawn board is ready to use, you'll have to joint one face flat, then thickness-plane it. The board you create through resawing must be thick enough to allow this.

You need flat, square surfaces as references if you expect to make accurate cuts. Flatten one face of your stock on the jointer. Joint an edge to straighten and square it in relation to the good face.

For resawing on the band saw, that's all the stock prep needed. For table-saw resawing, you need to rip the board to make the second edge straight, square to the jointed face and parallel to the jointed edge.

Keep in mind that if you're sawing a board into more than two pieces, you'll have to step back to the jointer after each cut to flatten the newly sawn face so you have a true surface to guide the next cut.

The resawn boards will, of course, need to be jointed and planed. Even the best blade won't yield a perfectly smooth cut surface. But it's best to allow them time to acclimate. Stack the boards with stickers between them to facilitate air float around each board, and place some weight on top of the pile. After a couple of days, joint and plane them smooth, flat and true.

The band saw is the main resawing tool in most shops. Its thin kerf minimizes waste and its capacity enables it to resaw wide boards.

Want ½"-thick stock for drawer sides? If you give yourself a decent margin for flattening the new boards, you'll get a single piece from typical 4/4 stock (right), maybe two from generously dimensioned 5/4 stock (right center), two comfortably from 6/4 (left center), and three pieces from 8/4 (left).

Because resawing exposes a new surface to the air, resawn boards often cup. These boards need to be face-jointed, then planed, dramatically reducing their thicknesses.

After resawing, stack the new boards with stickers for several days, to allow their moisture content to stabilize. Top the stack with a weighty object.

Resawing on the Table Saw

Need to resaw just a couple of narrow pieces? Turn, as I generally do in such situations, to the table saw. It's a snap to set up and it cuts quickly.

In brief, what you do is stand the board on edge and feed it along the fence, cutting it into two thinner pieces. If the board's width is less than the maximum cutting depth of the blade, that's all there is to it. If it's wider, but not more than twice the maximum cutting depth, resaw it in two passes, making a cut into each edge. If the board is wider still, make the two resawing passes, then use a handsaw or the band saw to complete the cut.

Being mindful of some details can help you achieve better results in resawing.

First, use a rip blade, preferably one with no more than 24 teeth. It's designed to do jobs like resawing and will produce a good cut without complaining. Combination blades generally lack the gullet depth needed to carry away the amount of waste created by resawing.

Second, use a featherboard. Clamp it to the saw table as close to the blade as you can without having it actually overlap the blade and pinch it. The fingers hold the stock firmly against the rip fence and prevent kick back.

Third, use a zero-clearance insert. Especially if you are making thin stock, a piece can tip into the slot in a standard insert. It can bind the blade, damaging the saw's motor. The piece can shoot back at you. Avoid trouble: Use an insert with a close-fitting blade slot.

One final caution: You can't use the typical American blade guard or splitter when resawing, so you won't have the protection they offer. Keep this in mind, because resawn boards occasionally warp and pinch the blade during the cut. This can literally stall the saw or cause a nasty kickback. Stay alert to the way your boards are responding to the saw.

I almost always stage resawing cuts on the table saw, making a first cut in each edge with the blade only an inch or so above the table. If the kerf does start to close up, subsequent cuts made with the blade cranked higher will open it again.

Need to resaw stock for a couple of small drawers? The table saw is standing by, ready for the job. Adjust the fence, set a featherboard and cut. You'll have the thin stock you need in just minutes.

The standard table saw throat plate has a gaping opening — primarily to allow you to tilt the blade for bevel cuts. When resawing, that opening is potentially hazardous. The thin stock you are creating can dip into it, stalling the feed and leading to kickback. Make yourself a plate with a zero-clearance slit.

Use a rip blade (right) rather than a combination blade (left) for resawing. The rip blade's flat-top grind cuts like a chisel, plowing nicely with the grain. The deep gullets in front of each tooth clear sawdust efficiently.

Step-by-Step Resawing on the Table Saw

1 Begin the first of several passes with the blade set fairly low. Set the jointed face against the fence. Use a featherboard to maintain steady pressure on the side of the stock and to prevent kickback.

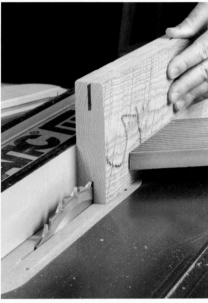

2 For the second pass, flip the stock end-for-end (so the jointed face is still against the fence). Make a cut. Both edges now are kerfed.

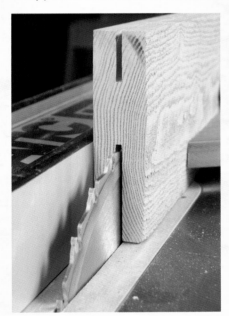

3 Raise the blade so it cuts a bit under halfway through the board. Make the third pass and deepen the kerf formed on the first pass.

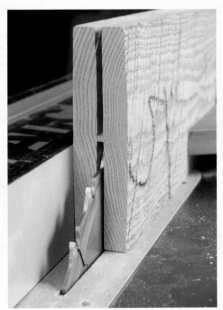

4 Flip the board again and deepen the kerf in the opposite edge. Just a thin web of wood connects the two halves. That web is easy to break, but it's enough to connect the halves so you can complete this pass safely.

5 Split the web carefully (so you don't tear fibers out of either face) and open up the board. The ridges remaining from the web plane off easily. Some saw marks are inevitable.

Resawing on the Band Saw

Say "resaw," and you probably think first of the band saw. Setup for resawing is fairly involved, but the results make it worthwhile. The band saw kerf is thinner than even a thin-kerfed table saw blade, so you don't lose as much wood to sawdust and you don't have to worry about kickback.

Setup starts with blade choice. For resawing, the right blade is wide and coarse-pitched. On my 14" saw, I use a $1/2$"-wide hook-tooth blade with 3 teeth per inch. If you have an 18" or larger saw, use a $3/4$"-wide blade. The hook-tooth grind is a little more aggressive than a standard grind and its deeper gullets clear sawdust well.

You're always advised to begin a resawing operation with a fresh, spankin' new blade, but you can go through a lot of blades if you follow that advice. I think it's sufficient to reserve a blade for resawing jobs. Don't hesitate to chuck it when it seems dull. Bear in mind that cutting curves tends to dull the teeth set to one side faster than those set to the other. The blade then tends to pull the stock toward the dull side. That's why you should reserve your resawing blade strictly for resawing.

The next steps are to check the tracking, adjust the tension and set the guides. Tracking is easy to check by turning the wheels by hand and ensuring the blade doesn't drift off the crown of the wheels. (While you're at it, use a stiff brush to scrub sawdust off the rubber on the wheels.)

Tension: I offer no guarantee, but what works for me (on my 14" saw with a $1/2$" blade) is to crank up the tension until the tension spring is almost totally collapsed. (At this point, the saw's gauge indicates the tension is right for a $3/4$" blade.) Then I make a test cut and assess the cut surfaces. They should be smooth and flat. If it appears the blade has bowed in the cut, I increase the tension.

When you've completed the resawing, reduce the tension. The saw and blade shouldn't stand idle with the tension cranked virtually to the max.

Guides: To cut accurately, a band saw blade must be fully supported on either side and at the back, both below and above the work. The saw has a set of guides just beneath the table and a second set on a vertically adjustable post you should set just above the work. Without them, the blade will deflect and bow as it cuts, producing a wandering, out-of-square cut.

The thrust bearings are positioned behind the band saw blade — one bearing above the table and one below — to prevent feed pressure from distorting it. There should be the tiniest clearance between blade and bearing when the blade isn't cutting. Wrap a strip of paper around the blade and adjust the bearing so it just kisses the paper.

A $1/2$" 3 tpi (teeth per inch), hook-tooth blade is what I use for resawing on my 14" band saw. The hook-style tooth is very aggressive, which minimizes feed resistance. The coarse pitch means the blade has ample gullets for clearing sawdust from the kerf.

The guides flank the blade, one pair above the table, another below, to keep the blade running true and prevent it from twisting. The guides must be set and locked just clear of the blade body. The conventional approach is to wrap a slip or two of paper around the blade and snug the guides against it.

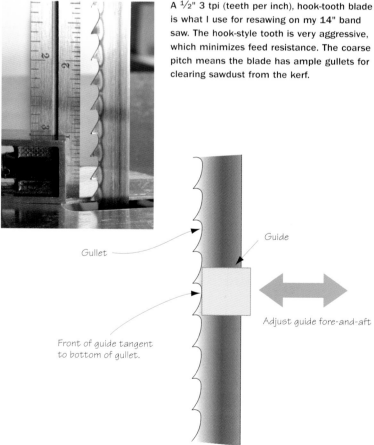

Gullet

Guide

Adjust guide fore-and-aft

Front of guide tangent to bottom of gullet.

Setting the Guides

Determine the drift angle of the blade by sawing along a line marked parallel to the edge of a scrap. Steer the workpiece as needed to cut on the line.

Setting the Resaw Fence

To guide your stock through the cut you need a fence that both provides good support for the workpiece and aligns parallel to the line the blade wants to cut.

The typical band saw blade doesn't rip in a line parallel to band's width. This phenomenon is usually called "drift," though some refer to it as "lead." The worst offenders are blades that are 1/2" wide or less—just the ones most used on 14" saws. The upshot is that if you guide the stock using the type of fence most common to home-shop band saws, you'll have problems.

The best solution is to make a simple plywood fence, as tall as the board you are resawing is wide, that you can align parallel to the drift angle and clamp to the saw table.

With a suitable fence readied, you need to establish what the drift angle is. Draw a line parallel to one long edge of a 12"- to 18"-long scrap. Start cutting and steer the scrap as necessary to cut on the line. Cut about 8" to 10", then stop and turn off the saw. Holding the scrap in place, capture the angle between the workpiece and the infeed edge of the saw table with a sliding bevel gauge.

Set the fence in position, and use the bevel gauge to establish the proper fence angle. Clamp the fence securely. Make a test cut of a short piece of the working stock. If it pulls away from the fence as you cut or requires excessive force to feed, check the drift setting again.

Cut about half the piece's length, then stop the saw. Hold the position of the scrap. Use a sliding bevel or the like to capture the scrap's angle in relation to the edge of the saw table.

Move the resaw fence into position. You can measure the gap between the blade and the fence with a rule, but gauge bars help you maintain the right gap as you adjust the fence to match the drift angle.

Making the Resaw Cut on the Band Saw

Start the cut with one hand applying continuous feed pressure and the other hand holding the board tightly to the fence. A featherboard can help; position it just in front of the blade. Keep a pusher handy and use it to feed the board through the final few inches of the cut.

Don't overdo the feed pressure. You want to work slowly, especially at first, and be alert to the vibrations and sounds made by the operation. With only a little practice, you'll develop a feel for how fast the blade can take the stock. When it's cutting at the optimum rate, the blade will barely touch the guide bearings. And when it's tracking properly in the cut, the blade's back edge will be centered in the kerf. If you are cutting a lot of material, the blade will dull in the course of your work, and as it does, the optimum feed rate will decline.

When you complete a cut, read the saw marks to evaluate your technique. A feed rate that's too fast causes the blade to distort inside the kerf. The marks it leaves will be deeper or shallower in the middle of the board than at the edges.

1 ABOVE LEFT **Begin a resaw cut holding the stock against the fence with one hand and feeding it into the blade with the other. Watch the cut; if it seems to be wandering, reduce your feed rate. Listen to the saw; with experience, you'll recognize what the saw sounds like when it's cutting well.**

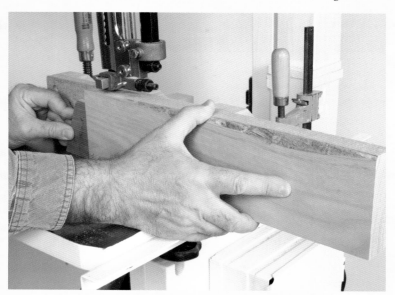

2 ABOVE RIGHT **As you near the end of the cut, use a pusher so you don't cut into your fingers. Reach around the blade to hold the stock and keep it from tumbling onto the floor.**

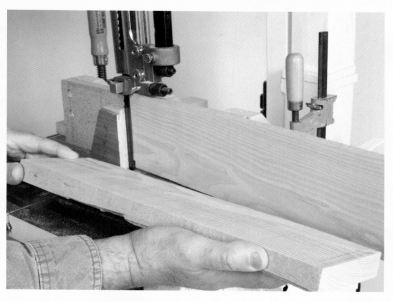

3 RIGHT **With the saw switched off, open up the board and assess the surfaces of the cut. What you see here is what you want — flat, smooth faces.**

Sheet Goods

Hardwood plywood is an excellent material for drawers. It is stable. It is strong. It is lightweight. A 4×8 sheet can be cut into a tall stack of drawer parts in a matter of minutes. No jointing, resawing, planing, edge-to-edge gluing required. So it's economical too.

I have used plywood for drawers supported on traditional wooden web frames, but I wouldn't use it where I expected to tweak the drawers for that fabled "piston fit." It's best used for drawers mounted on manufactured slides.

If at all possible, buy plywood for quality drawers from a plywood dealer, a company that supplies cabinetmakers, architectural mill-works and similar businesses. You'll be flabbergasted at the range and variety of what's available. Just don't expect to roam the aisles and pick through stacks.

To a dealer, plywood is any sheet good with three or more layers — an inner core and two face veneers. What is popularly known as plywood is, in the trade, known as veneer-core. MDF-core is widely used for cabinetry, as is MCP (melamine-coated particleboard).

The best plywood to use for drawers is the premium grade of veneer-core sold under names like Baltic, Finnish, Russian birch and Appleply. The 1/2" thickness is made up of 11 uniform plies, which are free of hidden, internal voids. Overall, such plywood is stiffer and denser than standard hardwood plywood. It holds fasteners better and makes better joints. The uniform, void-free edges can be sanded for a finished appearance.

Standard hardwood plywood can also be used but its quality is not as consistent. The 1/2" sheets usually have five to seven plies and the face veneers are very thin. Interior plies have voids, which can be exposed at the edges. The worst is the hardwood plywood sold at home centers. And don't think about construction-grade plywood for any but the roughest of drawers.

Various forms of medium-density fiberboard (MDF) and particleboard are used in cabinet manufacturing, but they aren't a good choice for drawer construction, primarily because they lack the grain structure essential for sound joinery. As one cabinetmaker I know says, "You can make a serviceable drawer from this material but not a first-class drawer."

Pre-finished plywood is available from plywood dealers. You can get it finished on one or both sides. The finish is a catalyzed coating that's a lot tougher than anything you can apply in your home shop.

Plywood is available with a finish already applied. Washable, stain resistant, and odor-free, the finish is as tough as it is shiny. And it shows off the beauty of wood. You can clearly see here the difference between unfinished and pre-finished.

The three basic types of sheet goods are (top to bottom), veneer-core plywood, MDF-core plywood, and melamine-coated particleboard, often called MCP. Any of these sheets can be used to build drawers. The results will vary.

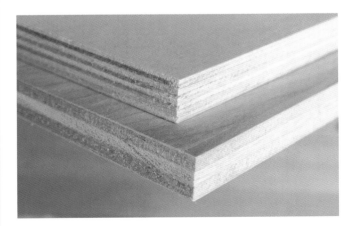

Baltic birch plywood compared to conventional birch plywood. Cost and availability are about the same, but Baltic birch is generally favored for drawer construction. It's curious (to me, anyway) that it's generally acceptable to leave the edges of the Baltic birch exposed, but not those of the conventional plywood. Perhaps it has to do with the uniformity of ply thickness in the Baltic birch.

Edge-Banding

"It depends" is the correct answer to the question of whether exposed plywood edges are acceptable in drawers.

Exposed plywood edges aren't particularly attractive to most people's eyes. Exposed particleboard or MDF edges are even worse. In some applications — drawers in your shop, in a basement or garage storage cabinet — you shrug off the aesthetics. But in your kitchen cabinets or an entertainment center, you're less likely to accept those raw edges.

An exception is the premium grades of plywood like Baltic birch or Appleply. The tight, uniform plies in such plywood are almost universally tolerable. Go figure.

Regardless of the material, those edges can be concealed under veneer or solid-wood bands.

Do the exposed plywood edges in these drawers look okay to you? Both okay? One but not the other? Neither? If you answered "no" to either or both options, edge-banding may be for you.

1. Shaped solid-wood edge-banding
2. Solid-wood edge-banding
3. Veneer tape edge-banding
4. 1/2" Baltic birch plywood
5. Standard 1/2" birch plywood

Matching the color of the banding stock to the face veneers is key in a successful edge-banding job. But so too is a gap-free fit of the band to the plywood edge.

Veneer Tape

A tried-and-proven edge-banding technique that's fast is veneer tape. A narrow strip of veneer with hot-melt or pressure-sensitive adhesive on one side, the tape is packaged in rolls ranging from 8' up to 250'. The tape is available in an assortment of wood species. You can also buy melamine edge-banding tape.

Use a special edge-banding iron or a common household clothes iron (no steam, please!) to press the tape to the edge and melt the adhesive. Immediately burnish the tape with a hardwood block, preferably one with a rounded edge. Trim the overhanging edges with a utility knife or a special trimmer.

Most often, veneer tape is applied before joinery is cut and the drawers assembled. It's easier to do. Obviously, you then have to be careful not to splinter the tape when you do cut the joinery. If you prefer, you can band the edges after assembly, though this is virtually impossible to do if the bottom is in place. But banding post-assembly helps you get tape joints that are tight and gap-free.

Line up the tape and press it to the edge with the iron. Move the iron slowly enough to thoroughly melt the glue, but not so slowly that the tape is scorched.

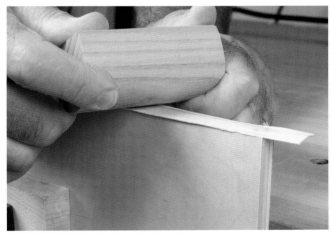

Set down the iron and without delay, burnish the tape in place with a rounded scrap of wood.

Trim the overhanging tape end with a utility knife (ABOVE). 2 or 3 passes with the knife will sever the tape cleanly. You can also use the knife to slice the edges of the tape flush with the faces of the plywood (RIGHT).

You can buy a special, inexpensive trimmer for veneer tape. The two-piece plastic body has a blade in each half. Pinch it on the edge of the banded piece and slide it to trim both edges simultaneously. It works great on $3/4$" material, less well on $1/2$".

Solid-Wood Edging

Gluing thin rippings of solid stock to the edges of plywood is the way I've edge-banded for years. And I'm sure I'm not alone in that. You get a thicker band than with iron-on veneer. Only a little more work is involved, and you don't need specialized tools.

My routine is to joint the edges of a board that's about 1/8" thicker than the material to be banded. I rip a 1/8" thick strip from each edge. Repeat the process if more than two bands are needed. By jointing the board's edges before each rip, the face of each band is smooth. Turn that face against the plywood. Apply the glue to the ply, then stick on the band. Use masking tape to "clamp" the band to the plywood.

The overhanging edges of the band can be trimmed flush with a hand plane or a hand-held router. My preference, however, is to do the job on the router table, as shown in the photos.

For what it's worth, solid-wood edge-banding would allow you to custom-fit plywood drawers. Though you wouldn't use a hand plane on raw plywood edges, you might on a 1/8"-thick band of solid wood glued to the plywood.

Gluing solid-wood bands to plywood drawer parts need not involve the usual gluing-and-clamping razzmatazz. Just apply glue to the plywood edge, set the band in place and rub it to build some tack, then stretch pieces of masking tape across the band and down on the plywood's faces. In minutes, the band will be secure and you can rip off the tape.

Trim solid-wood edge-banding with a flush-trim bit in a table-mounted router. Mount auxiliary facings to the fence so there's a narrow gap between their bottom edges and the tabletop. Set the fence tangent to the bit's bearing. With the plywood against the fence (TOP RIGHT), the edge extends into the gap until the spinning bit trims it flush (BOTTOM RIGHT).

A solid-wood edge band allows you to joint or hand plane a crisp, smooth surface on the edge. And even to hand-fit a plywood drawer to its pocket.

Shaped Solid-Wood Banding

A lot of woodworkers can't accept a plain old glue joint for edge-banding plywood. They just don't believe that glue spread on the plywood's edge will secure a thin strip of solid wood to the ply. They want biscuits or tongue-and-groove. So here are a couple profiles designed specifically for edge-banding.

I have to say that I was skeptical about these two-bit sets. I've had success over the years with thin rippings glued to plywood edges. In addition, I've used a proprietary system, the Burgess Edge, on several projects. While it works, it only works on 3/4" plywood. Moreover, adjusting the cutter to the specific thickness of the plywood you're working can be tedious.

I've got to say that I especially liked these V-groove-based edging approaches. You chuck the "plywood" bit in your table-mounted router and just center the cut on the plywood edge. Given the shapes of the cutters and the odd number of plies in veneer-core plywood, it's surprisingly easy to do. When you switch bits, you use a sample of the cut plywood to adjust the height of the edging bit.

The profiles give you a positive fit; you won't find the edging squirming out of alignment as you apply clamping pressure. Moreover, you get some long-grain to long-grain gluing surfaces, yielding a stronger bond than the long-grain to end-grain match you get with conventional glue-ups.

The edging has enough substance to allow tight miters at corners. And you can trim the edging very close to the plywood veneers without fearing the edging will de-laminate from the plywood.

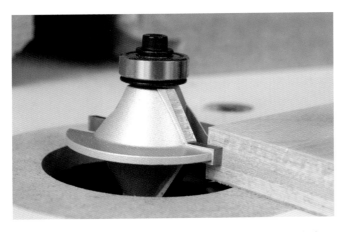

Plywood always has an off number of plies, which makes it relatively easy to center the edge-banding cutter by eye. This sample even has a center ply that's just about the same thickness as the groover, making it even easier. A test cut can be used to fine-tune the setting, if necessary. (Mark the sample's top face so you know which way to adjust the bit.)

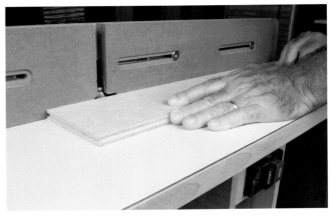

Forget the bearing; it's not a guide for setting the fence. Instead, position based on a test cut or two. The cut you want is in the center. The flats on the margins of the bottom sample's cut indicate the cut isn't deep enough; move the fence back. The cut into the top sample is altering the piece's dimension, indicating the cut is too deep; move the fence forward.

Use the routed plywood to set the elevation of the band-cutting bit. Tuck the sample beside the carbide tips and adjust the bit to align the notch in the cutter with the groove in the plywood.

A great benefit of the edge-band cutters is that you can thickness-plane the band stock to match the plywood thickness before routing the profile. The band will be flush, eliminating the need to flush-trim it.

CHAPTER FOUR

Cutting Joints

Joinery needs to be integrated into your drawer-building scheme. There are lots of joints you can use, as we saw in the first chapter; all produce strong boxes. How do you choose what you'll use?

Dovetails are the exclusive choice of some, but those folks are a parochial bunch. Dovetails are excellent joints, but you should choose joints appropriate to your overall plan — the piece that will house the drawer, the drawer's purpose, its mounting, and, of course, the materials. Dovetails in plywood? Yes, you can. But I wouldn't.

Dovetails are appropriate —even de rigueur — in fine furniture built of solid wood. Use them by all means in a fine chest of drawers or dresser, a sideboard or desk. But if you are building drawers to be mounted on mechanical slides, the joinery can be simpler. You don't need robust dovetails, for the slides reduce the stresses on the box — the yanking and racking and pounding.

Making a kitchen's worth of drawers? Hand-cutting dovetails to join them amounts to a punitive period of sawing and chopping and paring. Machine-cut rabbets and dadoes, various lock joints, or sliding dovetails are robust, visually agreeable, and quickly cut and assembled.

In the follow pages, you'll see the many joints used to build drawers and the basics of how to cut them. Choose wisely. And don't lose your perspective.

Fastened Butt Joint

Butt joints probably strike you as cheesy for drawer construction. Strikes me that way. They present a poor situation for gluing, and they lack any sort of mechanical interlock.

But consider that we often use butt joints to secure a drawer back between the sides. Though it's important to the integrity of the box, the back is seldom subjected to joint-wrenching stress. So we fit it between the sides, square it and shoot a few brads into the joint. Done!

Time is money, and there aren't faster ways to assemble straightforward boxes. Secured with nails, screws, or even dowels, butt joints do have satisfactory strength for drawers, especially if they're mounted on manufactured slides. The primary force on a drawer stresses its front-to-side joints. A butt joint will best resist the stresses if the sides overlap the front's ends, with fasteners connecting the two at a right angle to the force.

You see such drawers in economical kitchen cabinetry and in back-room storage units. In the former, an applied front conceals the end-grain of the sides, and in the latter, the exposed end-grain doesn't matter.

Fasteners aren't limited to butt joints, of course. Joints like rabbets often are secured with nails or staples, occasionally with screws.

Though you seldom see screws used in drawer construction, they're perfectly suitable. Drywall screws (RIGHT) are in virtually every shop; they're easy to drive and hold fine in wood or plywood. Conventional wood screws (LEFT) work well too. For melamine, use either hi-lo screws (CENTER) or confirmat screws (TOP CENTER). Both screws have deep threads, a shoulder beneath the head, and a head that is just slightly larger than the shoulder.

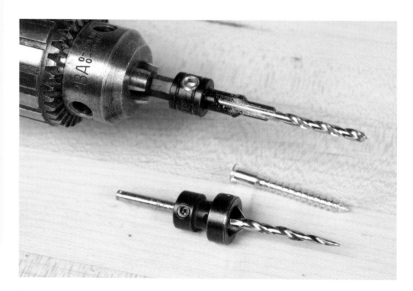

Melamine-coated particleboard (MCP) makes easily-cleanable drawers. Joinery is problematic, because it lacks grain structure. Try confirmat-style screws, specially designed for MDF and particleboard. A pilot hole penetrating both pieces is essential, and you need to bore it with a special bit (in the chuck) rather than a standard bit for wood screws.

Nails and Staples

Though nails are scorned by many woodworkers, there are legitimate uses for them in drawer building. A glued and fastened butt joint can hold a drawer box together for a reasonable lifespan. In the main, such joinery is used in kitchen cabinetry and the like, rather than fine furniture.

In production settings, where streamlined processes are essential, a few brads fired into a joint can immobilize it while glue sets. I've seen cabinetmakers tack drawers together with brads, then drive screws in pockets. Or assemble a drawer with biscuits, then shoot in brads or staples instead of applying clamps.

Pneumatics have penetrated even hobby shops, so nailing is very common. And almost effortless.

Position the tip of the nailer, squeeze the trigger, and it fires a brad — as long as 2" — into the wood, setting its head just below the surface. It won't split the wood,

either. Move the nailer to a new location, and fire another brad. Move it and fire again. In seconds, you can assemble that drawer.

Compare that to fumbling with clamps, trying to hold a tiny brad, and hammering it blow by blow. Maybe splitting the wood. Or bending the brad. Or denting the wood.

18-gauge brads are the least visible fasteners. Narrow-crown staples hold better, but are more obvious. You should fill holes, using wood putty in plywood or acrylic caulking in melamine.

Certainly, a hammer is cheaper, and it isn't tethered to a noisy air compressor.

Remember small finish nails? 3d and 4d sizes, even 6d. It's not difficult at all to hammer a nail into a joint, though in hard woods — oak, ash, hickory, birch, hard maple — you usually need to drill pilots. And you may need pilot holes as well in brittle species like alder and sassafras to avoid splitting them.

A benefit of pneumatics is that the fastener — whether brad, staple or finish nail — shoots into the wood in a split second. No hammer blows jar the parts, knocking them out of alignment. So you hold the parts together, position the nailer, squeeze the trigger. Pow! The fastener is in the joint.

Staples are more visible, but hold better than nails or brads. Adjust your nailer to set them, then use wood putty to fill the resulting depression, concealing them.

In the old days, woodworkers used hammer-driven brads and finish nails (above left) to assemble drawers (among other things). Nowadays, slender, chisel-tipped brads, finish nails and staples (above right) — glued into strips called "clips" — are fired into joints with compressed-air "guns."

Wooden Pins

Dowels, used like nails, can reinforce a butt joint. Assemble the joint, then drill holes and drive dowels. You'll have a strong joint, and the exposed dowel ends can be a decorative element.

To enhance the decorative aspect, you'll want to make some dowels from your primary wood or some other species that contrasts with the drawer side. A simple method for making dowels is to knock the corners off slender sticks by driving them through a hole in a metal strip. For my dowel-making die, I drilled a progression of holes in an aluminum strip.

Cut blanks as close in size to the desired diameter as you can. While you can hammer the blank through your die, I've gotten good results by spinning the blank. I chuck a stick into a drill, taper the tip to help get it started into the die, then spin it while pushing it through the hole.

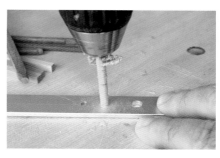

TOP LEFT   Taper the tip of the stick so it's easier to start in the shaping hole. With it chucked in your drill, use a pencil sharpener to knock off the corners.

TOP RIGHT   Spin the blank as you push it through the die. I lay the die over a dog hole in my bench top when doing this.

LEFT   Dowels made from the drawer-front wood reinforce a simple joint and accent its appearance.

You can turn out a handful of dowels in short order. Cut blanks from off-cuts and scraps. Drill holes in any piece of metal for a die. The die and your drill are the only tools you need.

Lay out and drill holes in the drawer joint (after the glue in it has dried). Apply a dab of glue to the end of a dowel and hammer it into the hole. Trim the excess flush with a saw or chisel and sand the drawer side.

Don't want to make dowels? Next time you shop for groceries, pick up a pack of BBQ skewers. The skewers will be made of birch or bamboo, and each stick should yield 5 to 7 pins, plenty for any drawer joint.

Pocket-Screw Joinery

Pocket screw construction is enormously poplar. Why? To borrow a phrase, "It's so easy a caveman can do it!" Too, the method is fast and reasonably strong. All the joints are fastened butts, but by locating the screws in pockets, they penetrate long grain, where they can hold better than in end grain.

I've seen two configurations of drawers constructed with pocket screws.

The most common, used in kitchen cabinetry, puts the pockets in the front and back, which are captured between the sides. The pockets are out-of-sight at the back and concealed by an applied front. The configuration puts the screws at right angles to the primary stress, which is good.

Less common is to form the pockets in the sides, which are butted against the drawer front. The rationale here is to integrate the show front into the structure, rather than apply it.

The screws in this arrangement virtually parallel the main stress's direction. That's not great, despite the fact that the screws are biting into long grain.

Moreover, it exposes the pockets. Yes, they can be plugged. But to me, that extra step negates the "quick-and-easy" benefit.

One caution: Don't be surprised if the screws completely penetrate 1/2" plywood, which of course is not quite 1/2" thick. Just the screw tips poke through. You can barely see them, but you sure can feel them!

While you can't cheat the guide block setting, you can set the stop collar on the bit shy of the location for 1/2" stock. The pocket will be shallower and the screws won't extend far enough to break through the mating part.

Though pocket screw joinery has gained a distinct identity, it's really just a fastened butt joint.

The pocket is formed with a special shouldered bit. The depth of the pocket must be tailored to the thickness of the stock, so use the gauge on the jig to set the stop collar position.

Constructing drawers with screws in pockets requires a drill and special bit, together with a jig to hold the workpiece and guide the drill. To locate the pockets uniformly on the work, lay out alignment marks on the work.

Stand the part in the jig, line up the pencil line on it with the appropriate mark on the jig, and lock the clamp. The layout has to be well away from the part's end or it will be obscured by the jig.

Insert the bit into the appropriate guide hole and drill until the stop collar bottoms against the jig. Pop open the clamp and reposition the workpiece for the next pocket.

The joint is a fastened butt joint. Apply glue and stand the part with the pockets on the mating part. Use the special locking-grip pliers to hold the parts. The post engages a pocket while the pad jaw seats against the bench's underside.

The screws are self-tapping. Though the pilot hole is bored as the pocket is formed, it doesn't penetrate the end of the piece. The screw cuts through and bores on into the adjoining part. Remove the lock-grip pliers and drive a screw in that pocket.

Biscuit Joint

For the uninitiated, a biscuit joint is a butt joint splined with a small beech wafer — the biscuit. Shaped like tiny, flattened footballs, they're stamped out, a process that compresses them. Add moisture and they swell up.

To make a joint, you cut a slot into each mating surface with a dedicated portable power tool, known as a biscuit joiner. Insert a biscuit into one slot, then slide the mating part into position. As you close the joint, the protruding biscuit half penetrates the second slot, providing a mechanical connection.

Using biscuit joinery means you build a box that will have an applied front. The sides overlap the ends of the structural front and the back. Slots are cut in the faces of the sides, the ends of the front and back. This orients the biscuits at right angles to the direction of the primary stress.

Not much sense in biscuiting the end of the side to the front's inner face. In that orientation, the biscuit offers no resistance to tension. The construction will probably work, at least for a time. But I wouldn't do it.

In biscuit joinery, rule number one is: Always use the same reference surface for slotting both parts of any joint.

A biscuit joiner has two reference surfaces: The base and the fence. Every joiner is designed to locate the center of the slot $3/8$" from the base. (That centers the slot on the edge of $3/4$" stock.) The tool's design virtually guarantees the base-to-slot-centerline dimension to be accurate. There's no adjuster built into the tool to alter it.

The fence, on the other hand, is designed to adjust. That means the adjustment can be "out." It can be misaligned with the cutter, you can misread the scale, the lock can be at little soft, allowing your setting to creep.

The upshot: My first choice always is the base.

It's easy to hold the tool steady when it's resting solidly and squarely on its base, less so when it's hanging from the fence. Keep in mind that the nose of the biscuit joiner must be square to the surface being slotted. If the slot isn't cut squarely to the surface, then the joint won't line up.

If the location of the slot must be shifted — almost always ways the case when making drawer boxes — use a shim under either the tool or the work. You'll find, as I have, that you can orient the work and the tool so you can use the base as the reference to produce slots for any form of biscuit joint.

On the workpieces, the reference surfaces should be those that must line up in the final assembly. For example, you need the face of the drawer front flush with the ends of the drawer sides. So you lay the front face-down on the bench top, and slot its end with the joiner's base setting on the bench top. To slot the face of the drawer side, stand it on end, braced squarely against a fence. With the joiner's base on the bench top, make the cut.

If the material is only $1/2$" thick, put a $1/8$"-thick shim under the drawer front or side, but keep the joiner base on the bench top (see page 79, top right photo).

A biscuit joint is a splined joint contrived specifically for use with sheet goods. Rather than undermine the integrity of the panel with a continuous cut, you make intermittent slots. In a drawer, be sure you capture the front between the sides.

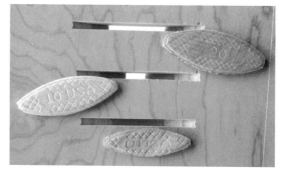

Be sure to match the biscuit to stock thickness. Most familiar is the #20 biscuit, the largest size (top). It's used in joining $3/4$"-thick panels into casework. But the slot for it will completely penetrate the $1/2$"-thick material usually used in drawer boxes. For $1/2$"-thick material, use the #0 biscuit (bottom). The intermediate size biscuit, #10 (middle) is for $5/8$"-thick material.

The working end of the biscuit joiner is placed against the workpiece with its red registration line on the centerline you've marked. When you switch it on and press it against the work, the cutter emerges and makes the slot.

Lay out slot locations at the ends of the drawer front and back. Prop a side on end against a fence clamped to the workbench, align the front against it and transfer the slot locations.

Slots are in the butt ends of the drawer front and back. Lay the part flat, end butted to the fence and cut the slot. Note the $1/2$"-thick part is on $1/8$" hardboard, the joiner on the bench top; the slot thus is centered.

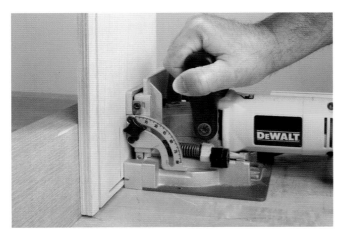

Slots are in the faces of the sides. Cut them with the side on end, braced against the fence. To align this slot with its mate in the drawer front, the side must be elevated $1/8$" — a strip of hardboard beneath the end does this — while the joiner is on the bench top.

Want to inset the back? Use a shim under the joiner to raise it in relation to the end of the side. Here the joiner rests on pieces of $1/2$" plywood and $1/8$" hardboard, while the side stands on the bench top.

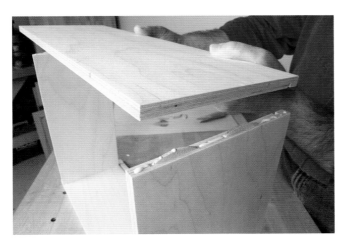

Begin assembling a drawer with one side on the bench. Spread glue in the slots and insert biscuits. Apply glue to the slots in the front and back and stand the parts in place. Apply glue, insert biscuits and set the second side in place.

Clamp the drawer box to seat the joints tight. Check the assembly for square. Leave the clamps on for a half-hour or so while the glue sets.

Rabbet Joint

One of the first joints tackled by newbie woodworkers is the rabbet. It's easy to cut and it helps locate the parts during assembly, but to be honest, it doesn't provide any more of a mechanical connection than a butt joint. Nevertheless, it's perfectly reasonable for drawers.

Because end-grain glues rather poorly, rabbet joints usually are fastened, either with brads, finish nails or staples. Screws can be used, though they seldom are in drawers. And dowels would make a good — and somewhat decorative — connection.

Good ways to cut rabbets abound. The table saw and router both offer several rabbeting approaches.

I prefer rabbeting on the router table, and I haven't yet built a drawer with parts too big for this technique. I select a mortising bit, which is like a rabbet bit without a pilot bearing. The fence adjustment controls the width of the cut.

The router can also be deployed as a hand tool: Immobilize the workpiece and move the cutting tool over it. In this mode, the piloted rabbeting bit is commonly used, though a straight or a mortising bit will work if you use an edge guide to control the cut.

Many woodworkers prefer rabbeting with a dado head in the table saw. You cut with the work flat on the saw table and one pass completes the cut.

Don't fret about the width of the dado stack, so long as it exceeds the width of the rabbet you want. Clamp a sacrificial facing to the fence and bury the cutter in this facing. To cut, you butt the work's end against the fence and feed it with the miter gauge.

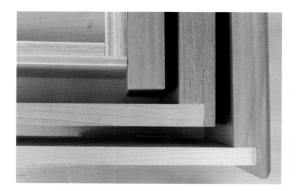

Rabbets can be used with any drawer front. Lipped and flush fronts are themselves rabbeted. Where an applied, overlay front is used, the sides are rabbeted to house the structural front.

Rabbeting drawer parts on the router table is efficient. Use a bearing-free planer bit and set the fence using a scrap of the material that will set into the rabbet. Use a push-block to back up the workpiece, preventing blowout as the cutter emerges from the good piece.

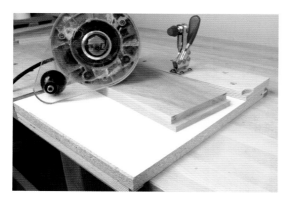

If you've got a lot of drawers to make, it can be worthwhile to make a bench hook with a toggle clamp, specifically for rabbeting the parts with a hand-held router. The fixture makes it easier to swap parts for cutting, and its fence offers blowout protection. The pilot bearing guides the cut and determines the cut width.

A dado head completes most any rabbet in one pass. Combine all the elements of the stack set on the saw's arbor. Clamp a sacrificial facing on the rip fence and expose only enough of the cutter to form the width of rabbet you want. Use the miter gauge to feed the work while keeping its end square against the rip fence.

Saw-Blade Rabbeting

A quick way to cut rabbets on a drawer or two is what I'd call saw-blade rabbeting on the table saw. Use whatever blade is in the saw. (The approach isn't quick if you start out by changing table-saw blades!)

Use a zero-clearance throat plate. On the second cut, the workpiece will be standing on edge, and you'll feed it between the fence and the blade. You don't want the work to get hung up on the throat plate.

The first cut forms the shoulder. To set up, adjust the blade height for the rabbet's depth. Next, position the fence to locate the rabbet's shoulder; measure from the fence to the outside of the blade.

To cut, lay the work flat on the saw table. Guide the work with your miter gauge, using the fence simply as a positioning device. It's easy to set up, and the miter gauge keeps the work from "walking" as it slides along the fence. No waste is left between the blade and the fence, so it's safe.

Now alter the setup for the bottom cut. This cut is made with the workpiece standing on edge, its kerfed face away from the fence. Set the blade elevation to match the width of the rabbet. Reposition the fence.

Yes, the cut can be precarious if the workpiece is big. A featherboard can help steady the work. Or you can mount a tall facing to the fence.

2 Reset the blade height against the shoulder cut to ensure you not only remove the waste, but form a crisp inside corner between the shoulder and base cuts.

1 Don't want to mount the dado head to rabbet one drawer? Cut those rabbets with the saw's regular blade. Set the rip fence to the width of the rabbet, remembering to measure from the outside of the blade. Set the blade height to the depth you want. Feeding the work with the miter gauge, cut the shoulder.

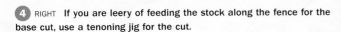

3 ABOVE After resetting the rip fence, stand the stock on end and feed it along the fence, completing the rabbet. The waste falls to the outside of the blade, so it won't kick back at you.

4 RIGHT If you are leery of feeding the stock along the fence for the base cut, use a tenoning jig for the cut.

Dovetail Rabbet Joint

The dovetail rabbet is an alternative to the more familiar rabbet joint. Simple to make on the router table, the joint comes together neatly and squarely. It's more resistant to racking than a conventional rabbet joint.

You can cut the joint with a single setup on the router table or you can customize it. The single-setup approach is a halving process. The same volume of waste is removed from each piece, so half the joint is on one piece and half on the other. If you want to remove more from one piece than the other, you are customizing the joint. Easily do-able, but not with one setup.

To cut the joint on ³/₄" stock, you need at least a ³/₄" dovetail bit. The ¹/₂" bit, which is the most common size, is just a little too small to give you a satisfactory joint. The bit's angle is irrelevant, since you use the same bit for both cuts. The bit's height is irrelevant to the fit of the joint; pick a height that looks right. The fence position is what makes the joint come together perfectly.

You cut one half the joint with the work flat on the tabletop. You stand its mate on end and slide it along the fence. When the fence is set properly, the bit makes the same cut in both pieces. What could be simpler?

If you want to change the joint proportions, you cut half the joint, placing the shoulder where you want it. Then you adjust the fence to produce a mating cut. On the router table, no bit-height adjustment should be necessary, just a fence adjustment. You'll have to find the fit through test cuts. But even with this approach, you cut one piece flat on the tabletop, the mate on end against the fence.

A dovetail rabbet looks just a little more stylish than the rabbet joint you're used to, and its zig-zag interlock resists some stresses just a little better too. The lower joint resulted from a halving setup, the upper from a custom two-part setup.

To rout the drawer side, stand it on end, inside face against the fence, and feed it across the bit with a backup block.

The height setting of the bit has little to do with the joint's fit. Put a sample of the drawer front stock beside it as you adjust the vertical setting and pick an elevation that "looks" right.

Rout the drawer front with it flat on the table, end against the fence. A backup block is important to prevent blowout. Make the other test cut with the sample in "drawer front" orientation.

Put the sample cuts together and assess how you need to adjust the fence setting. The left sample indicates you need to move the fence to house more of the bit. The right sample indicates you need to move the fence to expose more of the bit. The middle sample is right on.

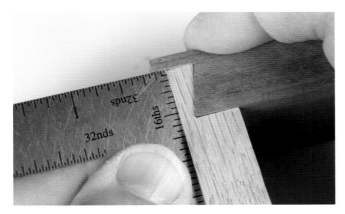

ABOVE LEFT Measure the misfit so you know how far to move the fence. In this case, the error in the joint is $9/64$". You must adjust the fence to back $9/128$" (half the total error) out of each cut.

ABOVE RIGHT Scribe a pencil line along the appropriate edge of the fence (the back edge if you need to decrease the cut, the front edge if you need to increase the cut). Loosen only that end of the fence and measure from the line as you reposition the fence. Any adjustment you make at one end will be halved at the bit, so you move the loosened end of the fence the full dimension of the error.

LEFT Though you've moved one end of the fence $9/64$", the change in the cut is half that. Cutting $9/128$" less from the side and the front yields a perfect fit. Go ahead and cut both halves of all the joints at this setting.

Lock Joint

The lock joint is one you've probably seen in diagrams of woodworking joints. It's a version of the dado-and-rabbet and a precursor to the routed drawer lock. For the drawer-maker, it's a joint with a lot of pluses.

• First of all it's a strong joint. The parts hook together mechanically. Glue alone secures them; nails or brads aren't necessary (though they won't hurt the joint in any way).

• The assembled joint is clean, with the interlock visible only from the top and bottom. You don't need to make separate fronts that are applied to conceal end-grain that's exposed to the front.

• It can join back and sides, as well as front and sides, which is important, from a production standpoint. One joinery setup can serve both ends of the drawer; it depends on the thickness of the drawer-box parts and the dimensions of the joint.

• The drawer front can be flush or lipped.

• You can scale the joint to mate different thicknesses of stock.

Scalability is beneficial. With the routed drawer lock, you have only one joint; the size is what it is, regardless of the stock thickness or the size and proportion of the drawer. The lock joint, on the other hand, can be tweaked to improve the proportions of the interlock. The width and depth of the dadoes cut in the drawer sides, for example, can be increased with the side thickness or the drawer dimensions.

The principle drawback is based on a misconception: Cutting it seems to involve a lot of setups. But the truth is that there are at least two ways you can cut the joint with one basic setup.

TOP **Open and closed lock joints.**

ABOVE **The lock joint can be scaled to suit a continuum of stock thicknesses, down to $5/16$".
The bottom drawer has a $3/4$"-thick front and $5/8$"-thick sides, while the top drawer has a front
that's $7/16$" thick mated to $3/8$"-thick sides. Though it's the same joint in both, the dimensions
of the cuts are dramatically different.**

A Basic Setup

You can form a sturdy lock joint on either the table saw or the router table with one basic setup and three cuts. The only setup change you make is to lower the cutter for the second and third cuts. Your stock must be at least ⅝" thick. The result is a flush-front drawer.

I'm always inclined to turn to the router table, because changing the dado set in the table saw is such a trial. In contrast, swapping router bits is fast and easy. But if you prefer the table saw, set up your dado cutter to ¼" and follow the same steps to cut the joint. You may prefer to use a tenoning jig to feed the workpieces when cutting slots (as opposed to sliding them along the fence).

1 Install a ¼" straight bit and raise it to match the thickness of the side stock. Use a ¼" gauge bar, as shown, or measure with a rule to establish a ¼" gap between the bit and the fence. Now you are set for the first cut; for the second and third cuts, you'll lower the bit.

2 Rout a slot in both ends of the front and back. Brace the inside face of the part against the fence as you slide it across the cutter. To stage the cut and reduce the load on your router and bit, stack several strips of hardboard on the tabletop; after making a pass, remove a strip to expose more of the bit. Use a push-block to feed the workpiece and prevent blowout.

3 Trim the locking tab next. Lay the front beside the bit, inside face down, and lower the bit until its tip is flush with the back wall of the slot. With the bit set, guide the front along the fence, using the push-block, and trim the slot's back wall. The resulting tab (INSET) locks the joint.

4 Dado the sides. Don't change a thing about the setup. Lay the stock on the tabletop and feed it with your push-block along the fence and across the bit. If you are using the same joint at the back as well as the front, dado both ends of each side.

5 Fit the joint together. If the joint is loose, you may be able to rescue it by tucking veneer into the gaps. But it's better to fine-tune the setup and recut the joint to achieve a snug fit.

Tweaking the Joint

The basic setup just described is appealing because it is so simple. But the joint it yields isn't optimal for all situations. That's why the lock joint's scalability is so beneficial. You can modify the dimensions of the joint, primarily by changing the thickness and length of the locking tab.

The basic parameters to remember: The slot depth in the drawer front's ends must match the thickness of the sides. (If you want a lipped drawer front, the slot depth must exceed the side thickness, of course. Just add the width of the desired lip to the slot depth.) The locking tab doesn't need to be thick or long.

A joint I use for drawers with $1/2$" sides has a locking tab $3/16$" thick and $3/16$" long. That places the dado $3/16$" from the side's end and limits its penetration to less than half the side's thickness. Used at the back, the joint becomes a dado-and-rabbet, which is fine.

I cut the side dadoes with a $3/16$" slot cutter and slot the drawer fronts with either a combination of slot cutters totalling $5/16$" — you have to combine a $3/16$" cutter and a $1/8$" cutter on the arbor to achieve this cut width in one pass — or a $5/16$" straight bit.

If, for some reason, a lock joint is imperative at the back as well as the front, then reduce the tab thickness to $1/8$" and place it $1/4$" from the side's end. The resulting lock joint will join a $1/2$" back to $1/2$" sides as well as the sides to a $3/4$" front. This dado can be cut in a single pass on the table saw or with a slot cutter on the router table.

For small drawers constructed of even thinner stock, slim down the dimensions further. The lock joint works fine with stock as thin as $5/16$".

An optimal joint for a range of stock thicknesses features a locking tab $3/16$" thick and $3/16$" long. That places the dado $5/16$" from the side's end and limits its penetration to less than half the side's thickness. Used at the back, the joint becomes a dado-and-rabbet, which is fine.

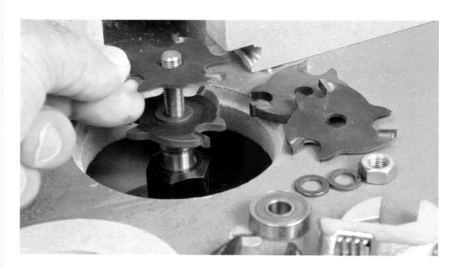

A slot cutter set is great for cutting lock joints. Cutters typically range from $1/8$" to $1/4$" (cutters as thin as $1/16$" are available from a few manufacturers), and they can be combined on the arbor when a wider cut is needed. The standard cut depth is $1/2$", but working on the router table without the bearing, you can exceed that by about $1/8$".

Lock joints can be cut on the table saw, using a crosscut or combination blade or a dado cutter. To cut the dadoes in the drawer sides, use the rip fence to locate the cut and the miter gauge to feed the work through the cut.

Slot-Cutter Magic

Here's a super system for routing lock joints with a $^1/_8$" slot cutter and just one setup. You set the cutter, position the fence and forget them. Each joint is cut in four passes, all with the bit and fence in the same position. To make the system work, you need two simple jigs: A $^3/_8$"-thick auxiliary facing for the router table fence and a booster sled.

The system does have limitations. The sides must be $^1/_2$" thick, no more and no less. The front can be thicker. It produces a flush drawer.

1 Here's the setup: Adjust the $^1/_8$" slot cutter $^1/_4$" above the tabletop and position the fence tangent to the pilot bearing. Clamp a $^3/_8$"-thick auxiliary facing to the fence, keeping it about 1" above the tabletop.

2 Cut the drawer front first. With it flat on the tabletop, inside face down, and its end square to the fence, feed it past the cutter. Use a push-block to keep the work square to the fence and to back up the cut.

3 Raise the workpiece for a second pass by setting it on a booster sled, which is simply a piece of $^1/_8$" hardboard with a fence glued to it. This pass widens the slot to $^1/_4$".

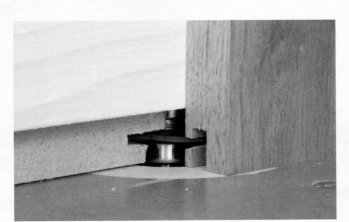

4 ABOVE LEFT Set the sled aside and stand the workpiece on end with the exposed face out. Slide it along the fence, trimming the slot's wall. This completes the drawer front.

5 LOWER LEFT Dado the drawer side. Stand the workpiece on end and feed it along the fence to make this cut.

6 ABOVE RIGHT When the parts are assembled you have a lock joint.

Routed Drawer Lock Joint

If you are feeling the need for speed in constructing drawers, the routed drawer lock joint is ideal. An interlock holds the front and sides together (and/or the back and sides) and it resists the main stresses administered to a drawer — tension, compression and racking. The finished drawer won't have the pizzazz of one assembled with dovetails, but this joint can go together a whole lot faster.

What makes the drawer lock so efficient is that you use a single bit to cut all the joinery for a drawer, including the groove for the bottom. You work on a router table, and use the fence to guide the workpieces. Dial in the height setting and forget it. Only the fence needs to be shifted between two positions in the course of the work.

Because the bit is small, you can use it in a low-power router and run it at full speed.

Though it's commonly used with plywood — particularly Baltic birch — to make boxes that get applied fronts, you can construct flush and lipped drawers in solid wood with drawer-lock joinery. Stock thickness doesn't affect setup, so you can make drawers with fronts thicker than the sides and backs.

Setting Up: Set up the router table and fence with zero-clearance inserts or overlays to minimize chipping and eliminate feed hang-ups. If need be, you can cover the tabletop with ⅛" hardboard and run the bit up through it. Likewise, you can attach hardboard to the fence with a couple of spring clamps. Put it in place with the bit running, and you'll have your zero-clearance cutout.

As a starting point, elevate the bit about ⅜" to ⁷⁄₁₆" above the tabletop. Slide the fence into position and adjust it so it is tangent to the small cutting diameter. Just the tab should protrude from the fence.

Make cuts in the edges of two pieces of the working stock, turn them over, and fit them together. While the pieces won't be flush, the interlock should be nice and tight. If it is, you've got the setup just right.

- If the fit is loose, raise the bit to tighten it.
- If the fit is too tight, lower the bit to loosen it.

If necessary, adjust the bit and make a couple of additional cuts to check the fit.

Once you have the setting, you are ready to make drawers. This setup is used to cut the sides and rout the parts for the bottom. To cut the fronts and backs, more of the bit must be exposed. Assuming you want flush-fitting drawer boxes, use a piece of the side stock as a gauge. Hold it against the fence and move the fence until the protruding tab is flush with the exposed face of the stock sample.

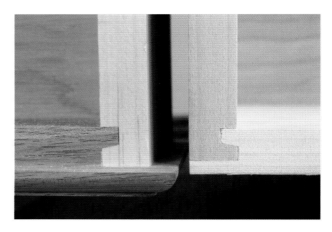

You need not limit your use of the drawer lock to utilitarian constructions. The joint works for lipped as well as flush drawers, constructed with all sorts of materials and in a wide range of stock thicknesses.

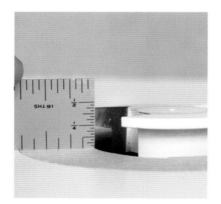

You've got to start somewhere. Use a rule to set the initial height of the drawer lock bit, then refine the setting through test cuts. The setting shown is a good starting point.

Tuning the Bit's Height

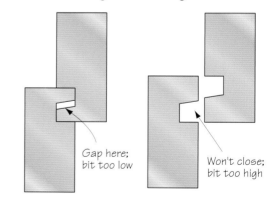

Gap here; bit too low

Won't close; bit too high

Positioning the Fence

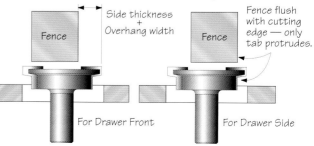

Side thickness + Overhang width

Fence flush with cutting edge — only tab protrudes.

For Drawer Front

For Drawer Side

Cutting the Joinery

Before routing, crosscut the parts the final lengths but leave them over-wide. Stock thickness has an impact on length. If you are using 1/2" stock, for example, the sides generally will be about 1/8" shorter than the desired drawer length (front to back). With 5/8" stock or with a front that's thicker than the back, the adjustment will be different. Make sample joints from scraps of the working stock to determine how much to adjust the lengths of the sides.

Leaving the parts a little wide is a practical workaround to the blowout that's common to cross-grain cuts. After cutting the lock joints, rip the parts to the final widths. You may opt to rout wide blanks and rip two or three parts from each.

Here's a workable joinery-cutting routine:

1: Rout the sides first. Stand a side on end, inside face against the fence, and slide it across the bit. Cut one end, then the other. I've never found a tall fence to be necessary, even with long sides, nor do I bother with featherboards. Do use them if you prefer.

2: Rout the fronts and back next. Adjust the fence position first. The work rests flat on the tabletop, its end butted against the fence. A square scrap used as a pusher helps keep the work moving evenly — and squarely — along the fence.

3: Stock thicknesses do not impact the fit of the joints. You can mix 3/4"-thick fronts with 1/2"-thick backs, routing all with the same setup. Cutting a front that overhangs the sides requires the fence to be set further back — add the overhang dimension to the side thickness and shift the fence.

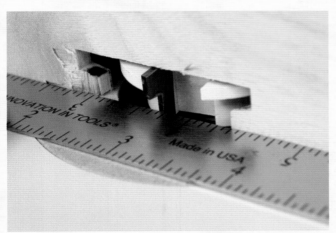

1 To rout the sides, set the fence tangent to the small diameter of the bit, leaving just the tab protruding. Check the setting with a rule. You want the cutting edge to graze the rule without actually moving it.

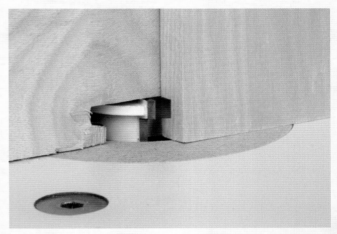

2 Stand a side on end, braced against the fence, and feed it across the bit. The zero-clearance fence's surface minimizes chip-out and prevents catches in the work's movement through the cut. To help stabilize the stock as you slide it (and further minimize tear-out) back up the work with a square scrap.

3 Use a scrap of side stock to reposition the fence for the joinery cuts in the fronts and backs. The tip of the cutting edge must be flush with the scrap's surface. This ensures the nose of the end piece will overlap the end grain of the side piece when the joint is assembled.

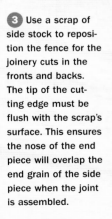

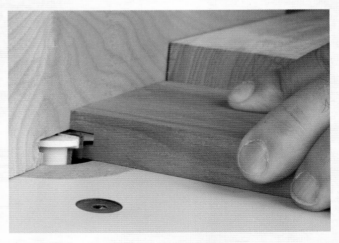

4 Lay a drawer end — either the front or the back — flat on the tabletop, its end butted against the fence. Feed it across the bit. Use a back-up block to keep the workpiece square to the fence throughout the cut and to minimize tear-out.

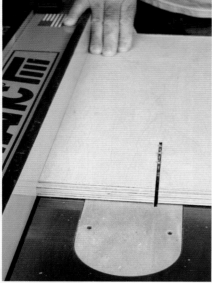

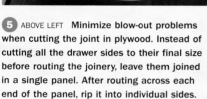

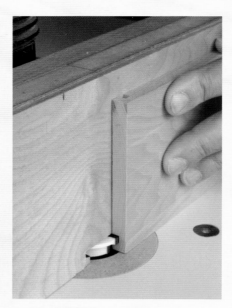

4: Rip the parts to their final widths.

5: Rout the groove for the bottom next. Return the fence to the side-cutting position. Cut from end to end. Because of the way the joints go together, the groove won't be visible.

6: Finally, mill the bottom to fit the groove. You keep the bit and fence setting as they are. Lay the 1/4" bottom material face down on the tabletop. The bit's protruding tab mills a chamfer along the edge as you feed the bottom along the fence. Cut all four edges.

5 ABOVE LEFT   **Minimize blow-out problems when cutting the joint in plywood. Instead of cutting all the drawer sides to their final size before routing the joinery, leave them joined in a single panel. After routing across each end of the panel, rip it into individual sides.**

6 ABOVE RIGHT   **After the corner joinery is cut, return the fence to the setting for the side cuts. Then rout bottom grooves in both sides and ends.**

Here's the fit you want.

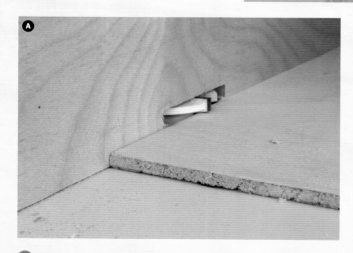

7 With the drawer bottom face down on the tabletop, rout all four edges. The cut will fit the bottom to the grooves cut for it in the fronts, sides and back, using the same bit.

Drawer Glue Joint

A seldom-seen variation of the routed drawer lock is the drawer glue joint. The cut profile has shoulders flanking interlocking tongues, the better to resist racking. Front and sides can be different thicknesses.

The joint is cut on the router table using a downsized glue-joint bit. The routine for setting up is slightly different than when using a conventional drawer lock bit, but the cutting sequence is the same.

I'd say the joint produced by this bit is stronger than a conventional drawer lock, thanks to that extra shoulder. And it will cut a glue joint on your solid-wood drawer stock (assuming it isn't too thick).

I've used two slightly different methods to set up the bit.

The first, shown in the drawing Primary Setup System, is presented by some bit manufacturers as the way to cut the joint. In brief, you set the bit and the fence to rout the drawer fronts (and backs, if you proposed to use the joint throughout the assembly). Then you change the bit height and shift the fence position and rout the sides.

The upshot is that you cut half the joint, after which you fiddle with the second setup to achieve a well-fitted joint.

Chuck the bit in a table-mounted router. Even a low-horsepower, fixed-speed router is fine for this size cutter. Raise the bit till the bottom edge of the notch is flush with the tabletop. (The rule is a visual aid in this instance, not a measuring device.)

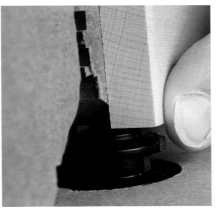

Use a drawer side as a gauge to position the fence for the drawer-front cut.

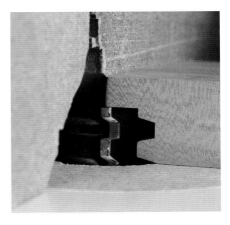

Lay the drawer front flat on the table, its end square against the fence, and make the cut. A push block prevents blowout.

Primary Setup System

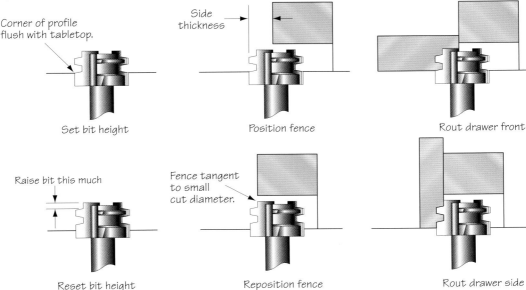

Corner of profile flush with tabletop.

Set bit height

Side thickness

Position fence

Rout drawer front

Raise bit this much

Reset bit height

Fence tangent to small cut diameter.

Reposition fence

Rout drawer side

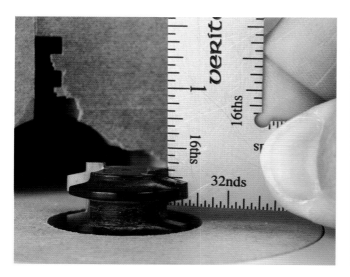 

Before you rout the drawer sides, you must raise the bit slightly and reposition the fence. Measure the height of the vertical flat at the top of the bit (LEFT); that distance is how far you raise the bit (RIGHT). Reposition the fence so the bit's small cutting diameter is tangent to the face.

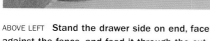

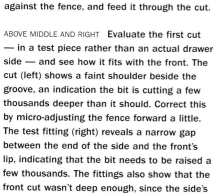

ABOVE LEFT **Stand the drawer side on end, face against the fence, and feed it through the cut.**

ABOVE MIDDLE AND RIGHT **Evaluate the first cut — in a test piece rather than an actual drawer side — and see how it fits with the front. The cut (left) shows a faint shoulder beside the groove, an indication the bit is cutting a few thousands deeper than it should. Correct this by micro-adjusting the fence forward a little. The test fitting (right) reveals a narrow gap between the end of the side and the front's lip, indicating that the bit needs to be raised a few thousands. The fittings also show that the front cut wasn't deep enough, since the side's outside face is proud of the front's end,**

RIGHT **After adjusting the bit and the fence and making a second round of cuts, the fit is perfect.**

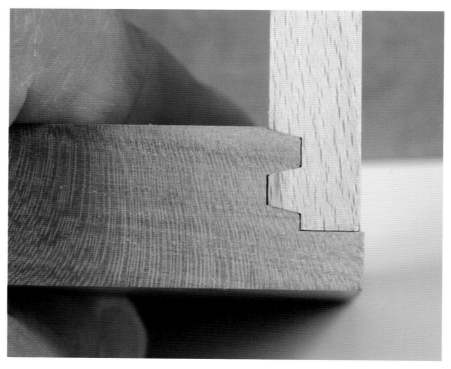

An Alternative Setup

The first time I used this type of bit, I had no setup instructions. Assuming it mimicked the drawer lock bit, I looked for the one bit height setting that would work for both the front and side cuts. And I found it.

The thicknesses of the workpieces have no bearing on the fit of the joint. The full setup sequence is shown in the drawing below.

Set the fence roughly between side-routing and front-routing positions. Make one cut with a scrap in the drawer-side orientation and the other with a scrap in the drawer-front orientation.

Fit the pieces together and evaluate the fit. A gap between the end of the "side" and the overlapping shoulder of the "front" means you must raise the bit. A joint you can't close means you must lower the bit. There is no "halving" going on here. If the gap is 1/8", then raise the bit 1/8".

With the bit height set, cut the joints. First, move the fence into proper position for routing the sides and rout them. Shift it back and rout the fronts and backs.

After cutting a sample representing the drawer front and another representing the side, fit the pieces together. If you can't, you must lower the bit slightly and cut new samples. If they fit with a gap, as shown here, measure the gap as precisely as you can.

Raise the bit by the width of the gap. My sample had a 3/64"-wide gap, so the bit must be raised 3/64".

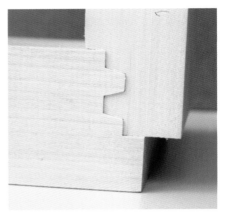

After adjustment, the test cuts fit perfectly. Now set the fence tangent to the bit's small cutting diameter and rout all the sides. Then shift the fence back, aligning it using a side as a gauge. Then rout the fronts (and backs).

Alternate Setup System

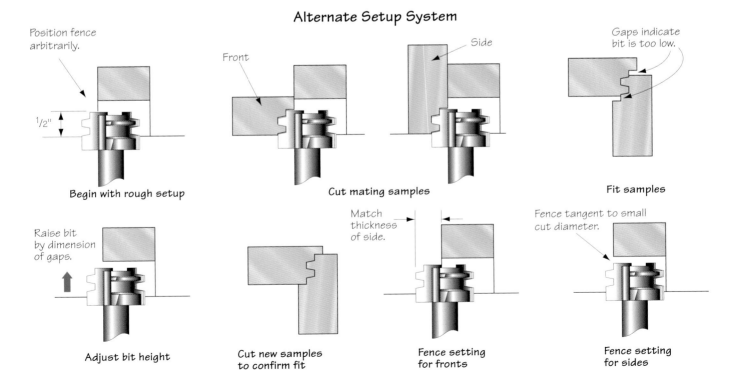

Position fence arbitrarily.

1/2"

Begin with rough setup

Front   Side

Cut mating samples

Gaps indicate bit is too low.

Fit samples

Raise bit by dimension of gaps.

Adjust bit height

Cut new samples to confirm fit

Match thickness of side.

Fence setting for fronts

Fence tangent to small cut diameter.

Fence setting for sides

Sliding Dovetail Joint

Dovetails are the traditional joint for drawers, but they're time-consuming to cut.

A sliding dovetail, sometimes called a French dovetail, gives you the mechanical strength of the dovetail, but you cut all the joinery on the router table.

To enable the outside shoulders to resist splitting off, inset the slots about $1/2$". If you need to provide space for side-mounted drawer slides, you've got it.

Use a $1/2$" dovetail bit in the table-mounted router. It works for $1/2$" stock as well as $3/4$". Adjust the cut depth to $1/4$". Set the fence so the slot's centerline will be $3/4$" from the end of the drawer front. Test it by slotting some scraps of the working stock.

To cut, butt the workpiece end against the fence, back it up with a pusher scavenged from your scrap bin, and feed the work from right to left, cutting the slot. Cut slots in the drawer sides for the back, and in the drawer front for the sides.

With all the slots cut, including a few in scraps, reposition the fence to cut the tails. Don't touch the bit setting, of course, just the fence.

House all but the very corner of the bit in the fence. Stand a side on end, face against the fence and cut across it. Turn the piece around and repeat the cut across the other face, completing the tail. Fit the tail in the slot in a scrap. Adjust the fence as necessary to get a tail of the correct size.

The sliding dovetail joint has two forms, either of which is great for drawer construction. The through cut (left) is the easiest to cut, and each time you open the drawer, that dovetail is displayed. The hidden form of the joint (right) is trickier to cut, is just as strong, but conceals the dovetail.

Cutting a through sliding dovetail is very simple. Set up the dovetail bit in the router table. For the groove, position the fence, orient the drawer part inside face down, back it up with a square-edged pusher and feed it along the fence and across the bit.

Switch to the tail cuts by moving only the fence. Keep the bit height setting exactly the same. House the bit in the fence, stand the part on end and slide it along the fence across the bit. Spin it around and cut the second face. Fit the tail to the groove and adjust the fence as necessary to achieve a tight-fitting tail.

Stopped Sliding Dovetails

You may want to stop the dovetail slots shy of the front's top edge so the joint is concealed, or so the front can extend a bit above the sides. This can be done, but for the best and safest results, make and use a sliding fence, as shown in the photos, to guide these stopped cuts.

The problem is feed direction. You can do the left end of each drawer front feeding right to left, which is the proper feed direction on a router table. But to slot the right-hand end, you have to make a climb cut, feeding from left to right, which is dicey.

The sliding fence allows you to make both cuts in the proper feed direction, and without changing the basic setup.

The key is the stop on the fence. You locate it to the right of the bit, because the cutter wants to pull the work that direction, and the stop resists that pull.

Position the stop for the cut on the drawer-front's right end. With the front's right end against the stop, you advance the fence and make the cut. Then reposition the workpiece for the second cut, placing a spacer between it and the stop. The length of the spacer matches the distance between the two cuts.

To govern the length of the cut, and to prevent you from the inadvertent through cut, you clamp a stop to the tabletop to arrest the movement of the sliding fence.

Let me be clear that withdrawing the work from the cutter constitutes a climb cut. There is a bit of risk as you pull the fence and workpiece back, so hold the work tightly to the fence as you pull it back at the cut's end.

Use a sliding fence on the router table to rout stopped sliding dovetails. Set a gauge block (or two) at the bit and gently slide the fence against them. Then clamp a stop to the tabletop to arrest the movement of the fence. In this instance, the cut will stop 3/8" shy of the drawer part's top edge.

With the drawer front braced against a stop block to the right of the bit, feed it onto the bit. The stop prevents the bit rotation from dragging the piece to the right, producing a curved rather than straight cut.

For the second groove, displace the front to the left with a spacer placed between it and the stop. The spacer's length must equal the distance between the centers of the two grooves. Note the movement stop clamped to the tabletop.

The tail formed on drawer side must be trimmed so the side's top edge will come flush with the top edge of the drawer front. When you cut the tail, turn the side 90° and, guiding it with a pusher, feed it along the fence, trimming the tail.

Box Joint

The box joint is a sort of square-cut through dovetail. It's used in the same situations as the dovetail. It has fair mechanical strength, but what it does is generate long-grain to long-grain glue area (the sort of glue area that yields the strongest bonding).

Look at a box-jointed drawer and imagine it dismantled. The ends of the parts are comb-like, with uniform pins and notches. The pins on one board fit into the notches on its mate, and vice versa. So making the joint is all about cutting a series of notches to form a series of pins.

You can cut the slots on the router table or the table saw with a dado cutter. Either does a clean job.

Whichever machine you use, the process is the same. Use a jig to position the work so the cuts and the pins between them are the same size. A critical part of the jig is a little key. It's custom-made, so it fits the cut exactly, and it's attached to the jig in a way that permits lateral adjustment so you can control the spacing of the cuts.

Most box-joint jigs attach to a miter gauge. The example shown here is independent and rides in both miter-gauge slots on a table saw top. It can be adapted to work on a router table.

The box joint has good mechanical strength and its many pins create lots of long-grain-to-long-grain gluing area. Thin pins are more work to cut, but they yield a stronger joint.

Table Saw Box-Joint Jig

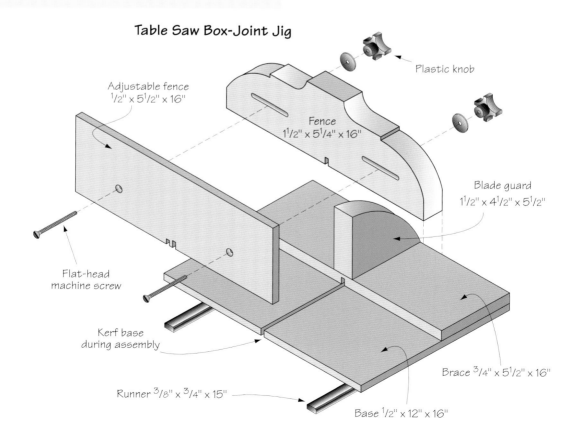

Adjustable fence
$1/2" \times 5^1/2" \times 16"$

Plastic knob

Fence
$1^1/2" \times 5^1/4" \times 16"$

Blade guard
$1^1/2" \times 4^1/2" \times 5^1/2"$

Flat-head
machine screw

Kerf base
during assembly

Brace $3/4" \times 5^1/2" \times 16"$

Runner $3/8" \times 3/4" \times 15"$

Base $1/2" \times 12" \times 16"$

The elevation of the cutter should match the stock thickness.

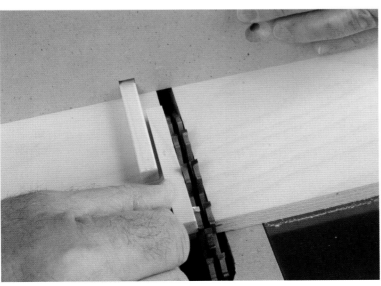

Using the Jig

You want to begin and end each array of pins with a full pin or notch. So the width of the drawer parts should be evenly divisible by the notch width. If this isn't possible, then it's best to change either the notch width or the drawer height.

A corollary is that a joint layout that begins with a full pin and ends with a full notch mates two identical pieces. You can cut both at the same time and all four parts of a drawer box can be cut simultaneously.

If the layout begins and ends with a full pin, you must cut the sides and ends in sequence.

Stock thickness has no bearing on the pin thickness. For example, you can use $1/4$" pins on $3/4$" stock or $1/2$" pins on $3/8$" stock.

But stock thickness does impact the pin length. The blade or bit elevation must equal the stock thickness (plus the jig base thickness, of course).

Set up the cutter and jig. Install the correct width of cutter in the table saw or router table. Adjust the cutter height against a scrap of the working stock.

The first cut you make creates a notch in the jig's facing for the key.

The next step is to make a key that fits the notch. The key must be the exact width of the notch, but no taller. Rip a stick close, then hand-plane it to fit. When it fits, clip it in two and glue one piece into the notch. The second piece is a gauge for adjusting the jig.

To adjust the jig for the joinery cuts, set the second piece of the key against the bit and slide the facing toward it until its key touches the loose one. The gap between the cutter and the key now equals the bit diameter.

Cutting a notch for the key (MIDDLE LEFT) is the first step in setting up the box joint jig. Make a key strip, hand-planing it to achieve a tight press-fit in the notch. Cut the strip into two pieces: one is the key, the second is a setup gauge. Hold the loose key against the saw blade as you slide the facing and key up to it (LEFT). You want the keys to just kiss, rather than jamming them together.

Cutting the Joints

There's no reason to cut the parts one at a time. It's repetitive, tedious work, so you'll appreciate anything you can do to expedite it.

As I already mentioned, if your joint layout begins with a pin and ends with a slot, you can cut sides and ends simultaneously. Four parts in a stack.

Align the parts in the stack, stand them on the jig base, upright against the back. Butt the edges against the key. Cut. Step the stack over the key and cut. Step again and cut again. Repeat and repeat until the last slot is cut.

If one piece begins and ends with pins, the mate will begin and end with slots. They must be cut in sequence. You can, of course, pair up parts of a box, but you can't cut all four parts at once.

Start with the piece that begins and ends with pins. Cut the slots in it. After the last slot has been cut, step that slot over the key. Stand the mating piece beside it, edge to edge. Cut. Remove the first piece and slide its mate to the right, the slot over the key. Cut again. Step and cut until all the slots are completed.

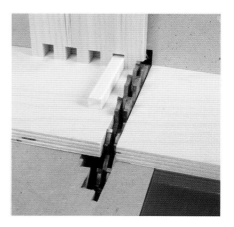

Stand the two pieces (only one is shown in these photos) of test-cut stock on end, tight against the key. Push the jig across the cutter and make the first notch (left). After each cut, step the work to the right (my right — it will appear as left in the photos), fitting the freshly cut notch over the key. Step-and-repeat until you've cut pins across the full width of the work.

Use feeler gauges to make fine adjustments. Where the pin is bigger than the notch, set a block against the key and clamp it. Loosen the facing, slip the feeler gauge between the block and the key. Relock the facing. On the other hand, if the notch is bigger, set the feeler gauge beside the key and clamp the block against it. Loosen the facing, remove the gauge and reset the facing with the key tight against the block.

Measuring the width of a pin and a notch will help you make a precise adjustment. Use dial calipers. Half the difference between the widths of a pin and a notch is how far you need to move the key toward or away from the cutter.

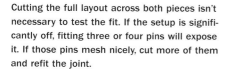

Cutting the full layout across both pieces isn't necessary to test the fit. If the setup is significantly off, fitting three or four pins will expose it. If those pins mesh nicely, cut more of them and refit the joint.

Tweaking the Setup

Stand a pair of samples in the jig, edges snug against the key. Cut a slot. Move the workpieces, fitting the slot over the key. Cut another slot. Repeat the process until all the pins are formed.

Fit the joint together (offset them if need be to align pins with slots). If the pins won't go into the slots, the key is too far from the cutter. If the pins are loose in the slots, the key is too close to it.

Rather than slide the facing left or right a "hair," or a "tad," or a "skosh," use your dial calipers. Measure a pin and a slot. The amount you move the facing is *half* the difference between the pin width and the slot width. You can use a feeler gauge to make precisely what is most likely a minute adjustment.

A second set of cuts will confirm the accuracy of your adjustment.

One note about fitting the joints. If your joint is long, with a dozen or more pins, you must be wary of cumulative error. A discrepancy of $1/128$" doesn't have a significant impact when the joint has 6 pins. But double or triple that number and you may have a joint that won't close. So the bigger the joint, the more precise your setup must be.

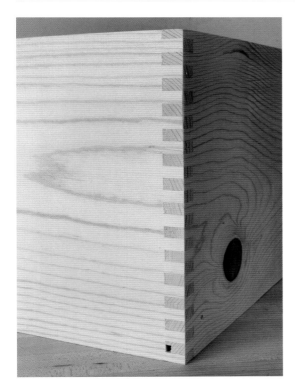

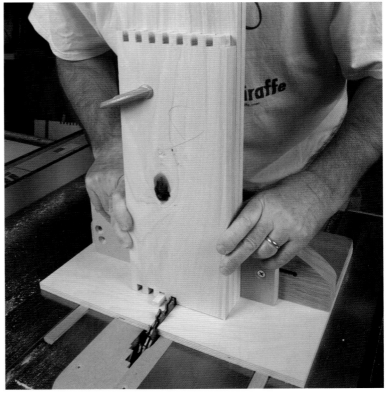

ABOVE LEFT In a joint with a dozen or more pins, be wary of cumulative error. A discrepancy of $1/128$" doesn't have a significant impact when the joint has 6 pins. But double or triple that number and you may have a joint that won't close. The bigger the joint, the more precise your setup must be.

ABOVE RIGHT When the joint on a piece begins and ends with a pin, you need to use it to begin cutting its mate, which begins and ends with notches. Step the last notch of the first workpiece over the key. Butt the mating workpiece against it and cut. Then set the first piece aside and continue notching the second.

RIGHT It's possible to slot several parts at the same time. This can expedite production. Note that if your joint's layout begins with a pin and ends with a notch, both sides and ends are alike, so you can cut all four parts of a box at the same time.

Box Joint Bit

This is a bit for cutting box joints in thin, narrow stock for tiny boxes and drawers. One pass cuts all the notches and tabs in the end of a piece 1⁹/₁₆" wide. Two passes (and a bit adjustment) are needed to form the joinery on anything wider — up to a maximum of 3³/₈" wide.

There's nothing to take apart or switch around or shim for fit. Chuck the bit in your table-mounted router, adjust the bit height carefully and rout.

Make yourself a pusher that allows you to support the parts on edge, back up the cuts and clamp the parts so they don't get pulled in by the cutter.

The width of your stock is critical. Perhaps the easiest approach is to rip your pieces as close to 1⁹/₁₆" as you can. Then cut the joints, assemble them and hand-plane the top and bottom edges of the boxes to make all the edges flush.

The box joint is great for teeny-weeny drawers or trays, but cutting it on thin, narrow stock in the conventional way can be tedious. A special router bit speeds up the work.

LEFT Each of the cutters is ⁵/₃₂", as is each gap between cutters. The first set-up step is to raise the bit ⁵/₃₂" above the tabletop.

ABOVE Because the joint on each piece begins with a notch and ends with a pin, the fastest way to cut the joints for a shallow drawer is to stack all four pieces and clamp them to your pusher — whether a sled that bears against the fence or a miter gauge. Two passes — one at each end of the stack — cuts the joints.

Assemble a joint. The pins and notches will mesh perfectly. The edges should be flush, and if they aren't, the bit height must be adjusted.

The width of the joint can be increased up to twice the bit's cutting height. The initial setup is what it is; stack your parts and make a cut.

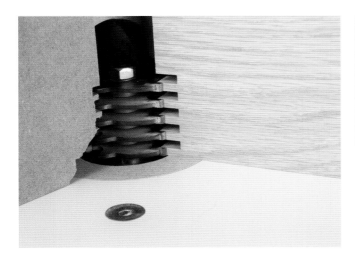

ABOVE LEFT For the second cut, you must lower the bit. Use one of the workpieces as a gauge, and adjust the bit so its cutters line up with the pins. Then turn the workpieces over and make a second cut.

ABOVE RIGHT AND LEFT The resulting joint fits perfectly.

Through Dovetails

Dovetails are prime joints. Long history, great appearance, cachet. Used in boxes and cases as well as drawers.

While appearance is important, strength is the chief benefit of dovetails. From time to time, woodworking periodicals test joints, and when it comes to case joints, dovetails always come out on top.

Through dovetails, which are visible from both planes of the joint, are used primarily between the sides and the back. It's been the joint of choice for that spot for centuries. You don't see it, but it bolsters the rigidity of the structure better than any other joint you might use there.

You can, of course, use through dovetails between the sides and front if you like the joinery exposed to the front. But half-blind dovetails are the primary choice there.

The rub is in the making. For many woodworkers, cutting dovetails the traditional way — with saw and chisels — is an insurmountable challenge.

Power tools can help, the most obvious being the router. Hand-cutting advocates like to argue that in the time it will take to master any of the router dovetail jigs you can master hand-cutting. (I'm not convinced that's true.)

On the other hand, I know of a couple of proficient hand-tool woodworkers who use routers and dovetail jigs, primarily to boost their productivity. In a drawer-making article published more than two decades ago, the late Tage Frid explained that he used a router and dovetail jig when building a piece with more than a couple of drawers.

Hybrid approaches are common. You can use a router to cut the tails and to waste the stock between the pins. You can cut the tails on the band saw. You can form the pins with a dado head in the table saw. Let's look at the principle ways you can do the job.

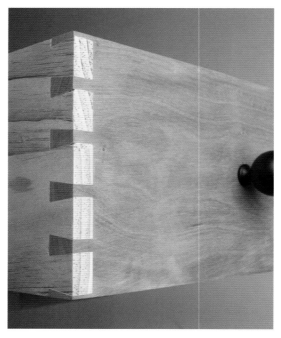

LEFT The reason that through dovetails are seldom used between sides and front is obvious. Unless both parts are the same species, you have blocks of contrasting end grain bordering the ends of the drawer front. An applied front would allow you to have the strength of dovetails, the cutting ease of throughs rather than half-blinds, and an attractive appearance.

BELOW At the back of a drawer is where through dovetails generally are used.

Hand-cut Through Dovetails

Hand-cut dovetails are storied joints. Mastering them is a woodworker's rite of passage. As with all such rites, chopping through the lore and myths is a big part of success.

Hundreds of magazine articles have been written about cutting dovetails. Entire books are devoted to the job. CDs and DVDs show how to do it. Neophytes often think there's a special trick to it. But it's largely a matter of sawing to a line and chiseling to a line. If you've never chopped dovetails, practice those two skills to start.

Start with the tools. Those required are modest in number, and you don't want to scrimp on quality. But you can spend hundreds and hundreds of dollars and be no closer to mastery of the job. You might be better served to use the tools you have and, as your skills improve — bolstering your confidence that, yes, you can do this! — spend judiciously on better-quality tools.

The essential tools include, of course, a suitable saw and chisels. You need a mallet to drive the chisels, though a hammer will do at the start. You need a marking gauge, a sliding bevel and setup gauge, a square, a marking knife and a sharp pencil.

Where to begin is a popular talking point. Pins First? Tails first? Does it matter, really? As far as I can tell, it doesn't. Whichever half of the joint you do first becomes a template for laying out the second.

What your array of pins looks like is up to you. The convention is to begin and end your layout with half-pins. The strongest joint is composed of pins and tails that are approximately equal in size — like the array produced by a half-blind dovetail jig. Many craftsmen like to use tiny pins — often called English-style dovetails. (Every woodworker will perceive them as hand-cut rather than routed, though they could actually be cut with power assistance, as we'll see.)

I admire Frank Klausz's approach. Rather than measuring and marking to ensure a uniform array, Frank cuts the pins by eye — no layout. This may seem cavalier, but it isn't. "You are cutting hand-cut dovetails," he points out. "There should be some variation."

Admiration aside, I'm more comfortable using a sliding bevel and pencil to mark a layout on the end of my pin board. I can erase a pencil line to shift or expand a pin or tail. Pencil layout accepted, I'll retrace the line with a marking knife and extend the lines down the faces to the baseline.

I'd suggest starting with a very basic layout, one with big pins and big tails. After you've mastered that, try a more demanding array with smaller pins.

Lay Out the Pins

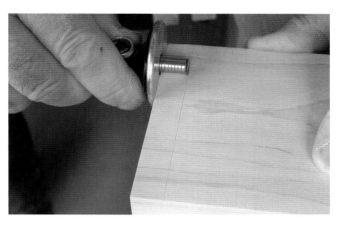

Set a marking gauge to the thickness of the tail board. Mark the baseline on the faces of both the pin board and the tail board. Also extend the mark across the edges of the tail board. Hold the work on the bench top to make it easier to scribe a deep, clean baseline.

Use a bevel set to the desired angle — 15° here — to lay out the pins on the end grain. Start with the half-pins at either edge, then divvy up the space between them by eye.

Extend the pin layouts onto the faces of the board with a small square and a marking knife.

Cut the Pins

The metal now meets the wood.

Two aspects of sawing give neophytes trouble. One is producing consistently vertical kerfs, the other is "sawing to a line." Some people use guide blocks, but that seems fussy to me.

Far better is to simply practice. Mark a baseline across both faces of a board and clamp it in the vise, end grain up. Set your saw on the near edge and start to cut. Saw down to the baseline. The goal is a vertical kerf that ends exactly at the baseline. Saw a kerf. Shift the saw to the side and make another kerf. Then another and another. Check your kerfs periodically with a square.

Another exercise may help you with sawing to a line. Scribe your marks with a scratch awl, producing a tiny V-shaped groove. With a dull pencil, trace over the groove; this highlights the margins of the groove, rather than its center. The exercise is to saw away one highlighted margin, leaving the other.

Working with a sharp chisel is the most significant aspect of chopping out the waste. There are a lot of paths to sharp edges and you've got to master at least one of them.

Too, you've got to accept that you'll never be able to drive even a sharp chisel straight through a 1/2"-thick hardwood board. You have to excavate a trench, so to speak, with one wall at the baseline. A common practice is to begin the excavation about 1/16" outside the baseline. It's easier to accurately pare to the baseline after the largest chunk of waste is removed.

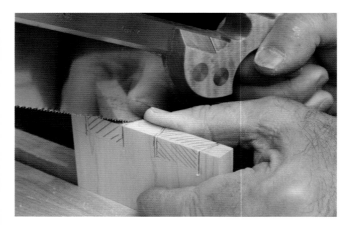

Use your thumb as a guide to start the kerf of your saw in the edge closest to you. After a couple strokes, begin to lower the angle of the blade. Saw down to the baseline, but no further. When you saw, try to relax and let the saw do the work. Use a one-handed grip.

Stand to the side of the work so you'll be better able to see that the chisel is square to the work. Use a relatively narrow chisel — 3/8" or 1/2" — so you have better control. Place the edge about 1/16" to the outside of the baseline. Be sure the chisel's perpendicular. Give it a sharp tap with your mallet. Work across the board, making this initial cut between all the pins.

Return to your starting point and create a divot across the waste. Set the chisel forward of your first cut (that is, toward the end of the board) about 1/8". Lean the chisel forward and tap it, lifting a chip. Again, work across the board, lifting chips.

Continue chiseling in this fashion. Pull the chisel upright and tap it. Lean it forward and tap to lift out another chip. Chop about halfway through the pin board.

Turn the board over and chisel into the waste in the same manner until you've completely severed it from the board.

Chop Out the Tails

Cutting the tails is more of the same sawing and chopping. Care is even more important now. Little deviations from layout aren't a problem on the pin board, but those same kinds of deviations here will show when you assemble the joint.

Critical is your ability to saw to an angled line. You've got to tilt the saw slightly as you cut. (Something else to practice!)

Chopping out the waste is where chisels with the ground-down edges prove their worth. They enable you to clean the acute corners between the tails and the baseline.

Stand the pin board on the mating tail board. The pin board must be flush with the end and edges of the mating board. I've clamped the boards together and it does free your hands. Transfer the pin contours onto the tail board with your layout knife. Go over the incised lines with a pencil so the marks stand out. Label the waste.

Cut on the waste side of the line with a dovetail saw. Use a guide block if it helps you align the saw.

Cut off the half-pin. A helpful trick here is to pare a V-groove at the baseline to locate the saw. The kerf should be just outside the marking gauge line. After sawing away the half-pin, pare the shoulder flush to the baseline.

Chisel the tails the same way you chiseled the pins.

If you did everything right, your joint should easily tap together.

Routed Through Dovetails

If you're of a mind to just power through this dovetail-cutting business, you'll find a variety of templates and jigs and gizmos for routing through dovetails.

These devices fall into three categories, based on capabilities: Those that cut only through dovetails, those that cut only half-blind dovetails, and those that cut both through and half-blinds. To gain flexibility, you have to accept a little more complexity. But there's more to the tradeoff than meets the eye, as we'll see.

(Actually, there is a fourth category of gizmos capable of helping you rout through dovetails: Precision positioning devices. These include elaborate fences for the router table (Incra and Jointech) and a kind of inverted router table with a hand-cranked power feeder (WoodRat). All have capabilities beyond mere dovetailing, and I doubt that dovetailing alone would draw you in their direction.)

The common denominator is that all are templates. A router template allows you to duplicate a contour again and again. So it is with a dovetail jig. Whether fixed or adjustable, all dovetail jigs are templates. You guide the router along the jig's edge as the bit cuts. You get the same contour again and again.

Unlike half-blind dovetail jigs, with which you cut both pins and tails simultaneously using a dovetail bit, through dovetail jigs require you to cut pins and tails separately, using a straight bit for the former, a dovetail bit for the latter.

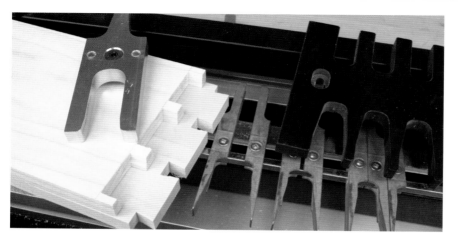

All through dovetail jigs are templates. Their straight fingers guide cuts with a dovetail bit to form the tails. The tapered fingers guide cuts with a straight bit to form the pins. The Keller template's fingers are fixed (right). The Katie Jig's fork produces a fixed-size pin; by varying the spacing of the forks, you alter the spaces between pins but not the size of the pins. The Leigh jig (center) has many split forks that adjust along rails, enabling you to alter both the size and the spacing of pins.

Tails are formed by cutting notches with a dovetail bit. A template guide rides along the template finger edges, thus guiding the router and determining where the bit cuts and how wide the cut is.

Pins are formed by cutting notches with a straight bit. The concept is the same as in cutting the tails. The template guide directs the router's path and the fingers control where the bit cuts.

Power Assists

Between the saw-and-chisel approach and the template-guided router approach is a dovetail-cutting realm where you control the layout of the joints, but harness your power tools to improve your accuracy and to expedite the cutting.

For a single, oddball job, that is often quicker than setting up a jig. Here are some techniques to harness your power tools for dovetailing.

Cutting Tails on the Router Table

You can initiate a dovetail joint by cutting the tail board on the router table. In doing this, you define the pins to match the size and angle of whatever bit you use. You get crisp tails from which you can mark out the pin board.

All you need is a router table, a miter gauge or sliding fence, and a reasonably-sized dovetail bit. If you use a miter gauge, you must attach a facing that extends across the bit axis so you can clamp the board to it to prevent self-feeding (which can mess up the cut) and to back up the cut to prevent blow-out.

The required layout is minimal — a baseline scribed with a marking gauge and a centerline for each cut. You mark the bit axis on the tabletop and line up the centerline with it.

Cutting Tails on the Band Saw

Cutting the tails on the band saw is faster and more accurate than cutting them by hand. You can begin a joint by laying out and band-sawing the tails, or you can band-saw tails transferred from a completed pin board.

A box-joint-type of jig can aid you in cutting tails, preparatory to hand-cutting the pins. Lay out the centers of the slots for the pins on the tail board. Align them with a registration line indicating the center of the bit and feed the work. Be sure you've got good backup behind the work to prevent tearout, and be sure too to clamp the work so the bit can't pull it.

Sawing out tails on the band saw is fast. Twist the workpiece so it's at the proper angle to the blade. Saw straight in just to the baseline. Make one cut on each tail before changing the workpiece angle to cut the second margin of each tail.

Nibble at the waste, taking your cuts almost to the baseline. When you've done as much as you can at the band saw, pare to the baseline with a chisel.

Power tools can help you form the pins too. Here I want to show you two methods, one using the router and the other the table saw. The router approach works whether you're originating the layout by cutting the pins or following a layout transferred from already-cut tails. The table-saw approach is trickier to use in the latter situation.

Roughing Out Pins with the Router

It's obvious that the router is great for effortlessly transforming solid wood into mounds of chips. It's no wonder that woodworkers use it to hog through the waste between pins.

The best of several approaches I've seen is used by cabinetmaker Michael Seward. After laying out and cutting the tails, Seward would transfer the layout to the pin board. He'd then use a plunge router to rough out the pins, doing the final paring and fitting with chisels. Because this was his regular routine for cutting through dovetails, he invested the time in making a dovetail-jig-like work holder.

Inspired by his example, I made a similar fixture. It's a time-saver, especially when making dovetails with those tiny English-style pins. In addition, I've found it's useful for roughing out the sockets between the pins for half-blind dovetails.

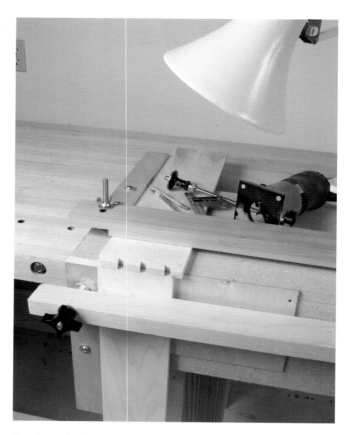

The pin-routing fixture holds the workpiece firmly for layout and for routing. It provides support and some guidance for the router.

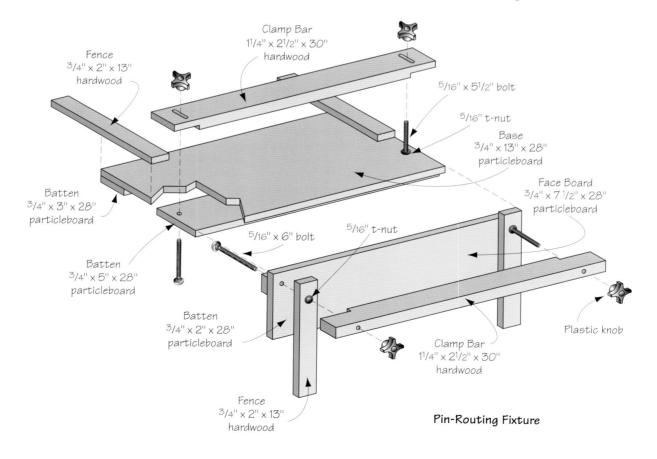

Fence
3/4" x 2" x 13"
hardwood

Clamp Bar
1 1/4" x 2 1/2" x 30"
hardwood

5/16" x 5 1/2" bolt

5/16" t-nut

Base
3/4" x 13" x 28"
particleboard

Batten
3/4" x 3" x 28"
particleboard

Face Board
3/4" x 7 1/2" x 28"
particleboard

Batten
3/4" x 5" x 28"
particleboard

5/16" x 6" bolt

5/16" t-nut

Plastic knob

Batten
3/4" x 2" x 28"
particleboard

Clamp Bar
1 1/4" x 2 1/2" x 30"
hardwood

Fence
3/4" x 2" x 13"
hardwood

Pin-Routing Fixture

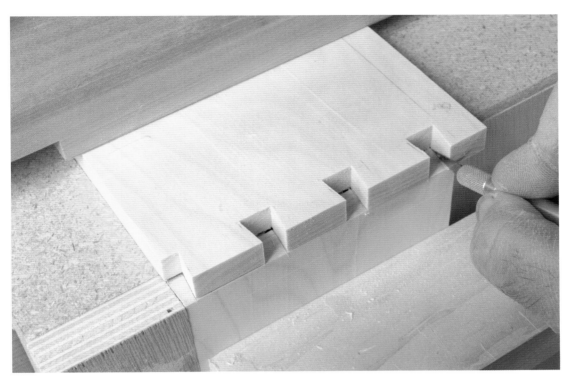

Clamp the drawer back in the fixture and align the side overlaying it. Slice along the edges of the tails with a marking knife. Then use a square to extend the layout down the face to the baseline.

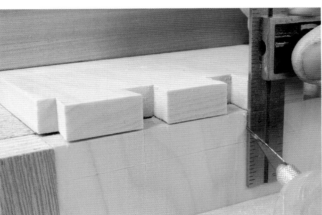

Set the cut depth to match the scribed baseline. Adjust the guide fence to minimize the degree to which the bit cuts into the backup board. Then rout out the gaps between pins freehand. Take small bites and plunge gradually, cutting as close to the knife-lines as you dare.

When you are done, the floor of the cut is uniform and clean from pin to pin. The knife lines are still evident, but that's evidence that you haven't overdone the routing. Minor paring with a chisel should produce a perfect fit.

Forming Pins on the Table Saw

This approach goes back more than 30 years for me when a colleague, Fred Matlack, built a blanket chest with through dovetails. He cut the pins on the table saw using a dado stack, guiding the work through the cuts with the miter gauge.

More recently I ran across an article that described the same technique, but using a dedicated sled rather than the miter gauge. A sketch plan of my version is shown.

The best application is where you are cutting the pins first and using them to lay out the tails.

Layout is simple. Scribe the baseline on both faces of the work with a marking gauge. The incised line helps prevent tearout. Next, mark the centerlines of the pins, spacing them any way you like.

Here's how you control the pin width. Pencil a registration line on the sled base beside each cutter slot (see the drawing). The distance from line to cutter is half the pin width. When you cut, align each layout line on the work with the sled's registration line.

Mount the stack set, combining cutters and chippers to produce a 1/2"-wide cut. Adjust the cutter height against the baseline on the workpiece.

The pins are formed in two rounds of cuts. The first round forms one side of each pin. Align the reference marks and push the sled across the cutter. Shift the work, aligning the next mark. After you've cut one side of each pin, rotate the sled 180° and cut the other side of each pin. If any waste remains between the cuts, shift the board, aligning the waste with the cutter, and make another pass.

Cut pins for through dovetail joints on the table saw with this shopmade sled. With a dado cutter set for a 1/2"-wide cut, you can waste the gaps between pins quickly. The angles of the fences determine the pin angles. Cut one edge of each pin, then turn the sled around and cut the second edge.

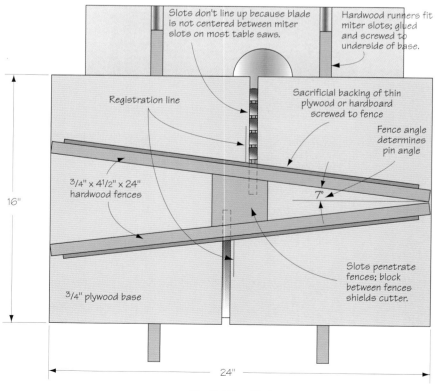

Slots don't line up because blade is not centered between miter slots on most table saws.

Hardwood runners fit miter slots; glued and screwed to underside of base.

Registration line

Sacrificial backing of thin plywood or hardboard screwed to fence

Fence angle determines pin angle

3/4" x 4 1/2" x 24" hardwood fences

16"

7°

3/4" plywood base

Slots penetrate fences; block between fences shields cutter.

24"

Pin-Cutting Sled

Stand the workpiece on the sled base, braced against the fence. Sandpaper glued to the sacrificial backing enables you to hold the work in place throughout a cut without clamping. Align the first layout mark on the board with the red registration line on the sled. Cut.

After a first round of cuts, you'll have a board with half-formed pins.

Turn the sled around on the saw and make a second round of cuts. As before, you align the layout marks on the work, one by one, with the registration line on the sled. The fence for this round of cuts is at a reverse angle to the first, so you form the second side of each pin.

After the second round of cuts, you'll have a board with fully formed pins. Depending on the distance between pins, there may be fragments of waste to trim off with another round of cuts.

Half-Blind Dovetails

The type of dovetail used most often in drawer construction is the half-blind. You find it at the front corners of drawers. When the drawer is closed, you don't see the joint. When the drawer is pulled open, there it is!

The dovetail consists of *pins*, which fit into triangular sockets between the *tails*. The pin at the edge of the board is called a *half-pin*, not because it is half as wide as the others, but because it slopes on only one face. Likewise, the tail at the end of the joint is called a *half-tail*.

The strength of the joint derives from two things: The interlocking pins and tails and an expansive glue area. The more pins and tails, the stronger the joint. Layouts nevertheless vary widely. A popular configuration among today's top furniture-makers has broad tails and small pins, which isn't the strongest setup.

Two design factors must be considered in laying out the joint:

Dovetail spacing: There's no need to space dovetails uniformly. On a wide joint, they often have close pins and small tails near the edges, which has the effect of putting three or four glue lines in the first inch of width, helping to resist cupping.

Dovetail angle: The slope, or gradient, should not vary. If your dovetails have too little slope, they surrender part of their mechanical strength and begin to look like the fingers of a box joint. If they have too much slope, the short grain at the tips of the tails will be weakened and may break off during assembly.

As is the case with through dovetails, half-blinds can be cut by hand using saw and chisels, routed with an inexpensive jig, and cut using hybrid approaches. Let's look first at routed half-blinds.

Routed Half-Blind Dovetails

The generic half-blind dovetail jig is the least expensive router dovetail jig to buy. How easy it is to set up is a matter of opinion. You clamp the stock into the jig, rout both the tail-board and the pin-board at once, and get uniform pins and tails.

The jigs consist of a metal base with a clamping system to hold the workpieces and a comb-like template to guide the router. The biggest difference from one brand to another, from one model to another, is the quality of the materials and hardware and the precision with which it's made and assembled. The cheapest ones have stamped parts that tend to flex and buckle, threads that strip easily, wing-nuts that chew at your fingers. The expensive versions have parts that are extruded rather than stamped or die-cast, big plastic knobs instead of wing-nuts and a measure of adjustability. Some even have additional templates, that let you cut 1/4" half-blind dovetails in addition to the standard 1/2" variety, and 1/4" and 1/2" box joints as well.

In addition to the jig, you need a router, a dovetail bit (usually the 1/2", 14° variety), and a guide bushing (usually one with a 7/16" outside diameter, which limits you to a 1/4" shank bit). The best router to use is a 1- or 1 1/2-horsepower fixed-base model. The ability to plunge is irrelevant in this operation and brute power doesn't contribute much — if anything.

1 RIGHT **These routed half-blind dovetails, once the jig is set up properly, can be cut quickly and the results will be consistent each and every time.**

2 BELOW **The typical half-blind dovetail jig cuts both pins and tails at the same time with the same bit. This one has an extruded aluminum base, phenolic template and large knobs. I mounted it on a platform to expand workpiece support and extend the positioning fences on the front and the top.**

For the sake of appearance (it won't affect the strength of the joint), you want to begin and end with a half pin. But machine-cut half-blind dovetails are inflexible. You can't alter their size to distribute them evenly across the width of board you're working with. What you have to do is alter the width of the board.

The 1/2" dovetail lays out on 7/8" centers. That is, the distance from the center of one pin to the center of the next is 7/8". So, as the drawing shows, you should try to adjust the width of the work to achieve even spacing

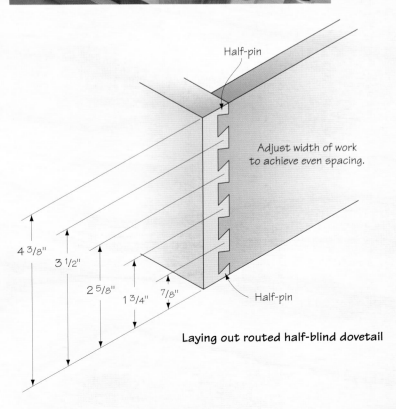

Half-pin

Adjust width of work to achieve even spacing.

4 3/8"

3 1/2"

2 5/8"

1 3/4"   7/8"

Half-pin

Laying out routed half-blind dovetail

Setting Up the Jig and Router

Install the $7/16$" guide bushing in the baseplate. Then adjust the router so the collet is relatively close to the bushing and carefully insert the $1/4$" shank bit. Tighten the collet nut.

Adjust the depth of cut next. The usual setting is $1/2$", though your jig's instructions may specify some other figure.

Set up the jig. The workpieces have to be clamped in the jig in a particular way. The drawer front is clamped to the top of the jig, inner face up. The drawer side is clamped to the front of the jig, inside face out. The front must be butted against the face of the side. The end of the side must be flush with the top surface of the front.

Here's the easiest way to do it. Roughly position the side in the jig with its top end well above the jig. Slide the front under the top clamp bar and butt it tightly against the side. Screw down the clamp bar.

Now loosen the clamp bar holding the side and lower it until its end is flush with the other workpiece. Re-clamp it firmly.

Both pieces need to be against the alignment pins or stops. These stops align the two workpieces so their edges are offset exactly $7/16$". This is the amount they must be off-set so the edges of the assembled joint will be flush. Every jig has a pair of these stops at either end.

Fit the template in place next. If you have a choice, adjust it so it will yield a flush dovetail. The template needs to be flat on the workpieces and the hold-fast cinched tightly.

Half-Blind Dovetails
Setting Depth-of-Cut

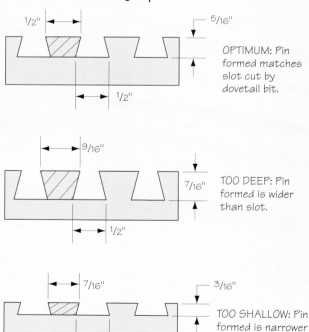

OPTIMUM: Pin formed matches slot cut by dovetail bit.

TOO DEEP: Pin formed is wider than slot.

TOO SHALLOW: Pin formed is narrower than slot.

3 Use a small machinist's square to set the bit extension. Remember to account for the template thickness. Once the bit is set, turn it by hand to be absolutely sure it doesn't contact the bushing (which will damage the bit's carbide).

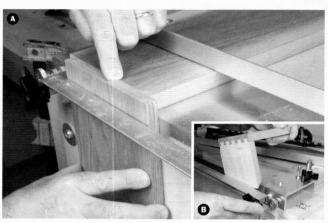

4 Line up the workpieces carefully as you clamp them in the jig. Both must be snug against the guide pins. Snug the end of the drawer front (it's on top) against the inner face of the drawer side (it's on the front). Make sure the pieces are flush. Fit a spacer (made of scraps from the working stock) into the unused side of the jig (INSET), both to balance the clamping pressure and keep the template from sagging,

5 On most jigs, the template is attached to a pair of L-shaped forked brackets. The forks drop onto studs projecting from the jig chassis. Nuts on the studs adjust the fore-and-aft position of the template; this adjustment controls how deep the tails penetrate the sockets. Turn the nuts in to increase the socket depth, out to decrease it (INSET).

6 Chipping along the shoulder of the tail piece can be a distinct problem. Try making a shallow cut to establish the shoulder before routing the dovetails. A climb cut — where you feed the router from right to left — is most effective here.

7 Routing the tails and sockets takes a matter of seconds. Feed the router into each slot. Keep the template guide tight against the template as you come out of one slot and round the finger into the next slot.

8 With the cut complete, pop off the template and take a good look at the cut. If you see a little bump on a tail, or that you failed to get a socket cut to the full depth, you can usually replace the template and recut those spots.

Cutting a Test Joint

Rout the dovetails, slot by slot, beginning on the left and working to the right. You may want to zip back through them when you are done, just to be sure you didn't pull out of a slot too soon, leaving the work only partially cut.

Cut the power and pull the router toward you, clear of the jig. Take a good look at the work and be sure you haven't missed a spot. (If you have, rout it now, before moving anything.) Only then should you remove the work and test-assemble the joint.

Chances are, your setup needs a little fine tuning.

Fit too tight? The bit's cutting too deep. Reduce the depth of cut slightly.

Fit too loose? The bit's not cutting deep enough. Increase the depth of cut slightly.

Sockets too shallow or too deep? The template is misaligned. To reduce the socket depth, move the template very slightly toward you. To increase the socket depth, move the template away from you.

Any other problems you have will stem from misalignment of the workpieces in the jig. Make sure the top surface of the socket piece is flush with the top end of the tail piece, that they are at right angles to each other, that the template is square to the workpieces, and so forth.

When you've successfully fine-tuned the setup using the alignment pins on the left, cut a test joint using the right end of the jig. Do any additional tuning needed there.

9 Your first joint may not fit exactly the way you want it to. The nature of the misfit cues you to how to correct it on your next cut. If the tails don't fit into the sockets (left), you must reduce the cutting depth. If the tails are loose in the sockets (center), you must increase the cutting depth. If the tails fit the sockets, but penetrate too deeply or not deeply enough (right), you must adjust the fore-and-after position of the template.

Cutting the Good Stuff

Before starting on the good wood, make sure you're organized for complete success. It doesn't matter if you are dovetailing one drawer or fifty drawers, it's all too easy to get mixed-up and cut the dovetails in the wrong places.

Do this. Label the parts on what will be their inside faces. If you can read the labels when the parts are in the jig, you've got the orientation correct. If you are doing drawers, the sides always go on the front, and the fronts and backs always go on the top.

And you need to label more than part names. Consider that each drawer or box has four joints. When you are doing machine-cut dovetails, two of the four joints must be cut on the left side of the jig and two on the right side. You don't want to get them mixed up.

A good system is shown in the drawing. The labels are put on the inner face, the one that's up in the jig. The letters are always associated with a particular part. Each letter is placed at the bottom edge of the piece, to indicate which edge goes against the jig's alignment stops. On the jig itself, you mark two two-letter combinations beside each pair of alignment stops, as indicated in the drawing. As you clamp the parts into the jig, orient the letters toward the stops, and check the combination. If it isn't on your list of two, you are at the wrong end of the jig.

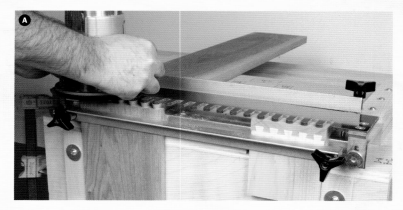

10 Dovetail jigs are handed. The top edges of your parts must always be oriented to the outside, with the inner surfaces exposed. Thus, the joints on the left of your assembly must be cut on the left end of the jig (TOP), while the right side joints must be cut on the jig's right (BOTTOM). Methodically marking the parts, as well as drawing a setup diagram on the jig, can reduce goof-ups that waste materials and time.

Organizing the Parts

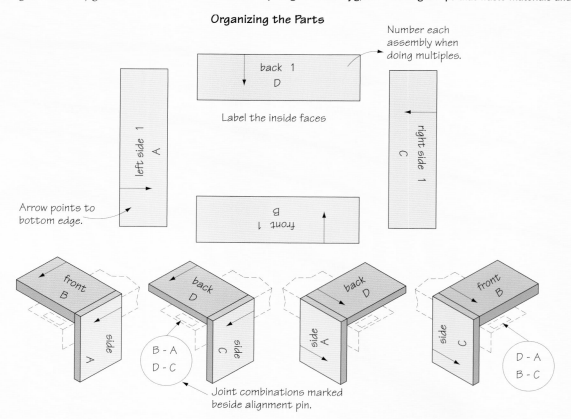

Number each assembly when doing multiples.

back 1
D

Label the inside faces

left side 1
A

right side 1
C

Arrow points to bottom edge.

front 1
B

front
B

side
A

back
D

side
C

B - A
D - C

side
A

back
D

side
C

front
B

D - A
B - C

Joint combinations marked beside alignment pin.

Variably Spaced Half-Blinds

The rap on routed half-blind dovetails is the rigidity of the layout. Yes, the joints can be zipped out. The size and arrangement of pins and tails is ideal for strength. But having to proportion your drawers to suit the technology rather than your own aesthetics is disappointing.

At least three brands of dovetail jigs — Leigh, Akeda, and Omnijig (which now appears to be a clone of the Leigh) — enable to you to vary the size and spacing of pins and tails in half-blinds. The pin cannot, of course, be less than the size of your dovetail bit. But you do control number and spacing of the pins. And that changes the size of the tails.

This has the benefit of allowing you to customize your dovetail layouts to the drawer sizes.

But the primary benefit is, baldly, cosmetic. The joints you make aren't stronger. But most observers will be less certain that you routed them.

1 So maybe it isn't as strong as common-place routed half-blinds. I think it looks better and it's plenty strong for this drawer.

2 The Leigh jig's individual guide fingers slide along two bars and are locked in position with a square-drive screw. Set them by eye or with a rule.

3 Cut the tails with the drawer side clamped vertically in the front of the jig, a spoilboard clamped tight against the side, and the guide-finger assembly oriented with the round-tipped fingers to the front. If the tails are wide, as here, shopmade bridge strips should be used to prevent mis-routing.

4 Rout the sockets in the drawer front with it clamped on top of the jig. A scrap clamped to the jig front aligns the workpiece without interfering with the cut. Flip the guide-finger assembly so the pointed ends of the fingers are to the front.

Rabbeted Half-Blinds

You can dovetail a lipped drawer with any half-blind dovetail jig. The tricks are to dovetail the front separately from the sides and to clamp it forward of its usual position. You can accommodate most any width of rabbet. Here's how.

Rough out the drawer parts, and rabbet the fronts. At the same time, cut some scraps the same thickness as the drawer fronts to back up the sides when routing the tails. Also cut a scrap to position the fronts in the jig. This alignment gauge needs a rabbet across one end that's identical to the drawer-front rabbet.

Finally, you need a spacer to offset the drawer front from the alignment stop so the first socket is a half-pin from the shoulder of the rabbet. To determine how thick the spacer must be, subtract the width of the drawer-front rabbet from $7/8$", the center-to-center spacing of $1/2$" dovetails. If the rabbet is $3/8$", for example, you need a $1/2$" spacer.

Rout the sockets in the drawer fronts first. Clamp the alignment gauge in the jig in place of the drawer side. Set the spacer against the alignment stop, then set the drawer front in the jig, as shown in the drawing. Butt the end against the tab of the alignment gauge, the bottom edge against the spacer. Clamp the front, then rout the sockets.

Naturally, you have to switch to the other end of the jig to rout the sockets in the other end of the drawer front.

After the sockets are routed, fit the drawer sides in place, one by one, and rout the tails. To help you position each side, and to prevent tearout, clamp a scrap in the jig in place of the drawer front.

Routing Rabbeted Half-Blind Dovetails

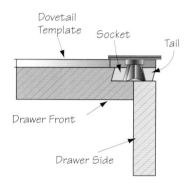

A Flush Dovetail
Tail and socket routed simultaneously

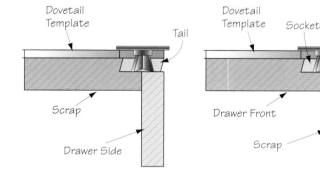

A Rabbeted Dovetail
Routing the tail   Routing the socket

ABOVE **The setup logic for routing rabbeted half-blind dovetails is evident here. When the jig is set up for routing a flush joint (left), the template overlays the front and side more or less equally. The socket depth therefore will match the tail thickness.**

When you rout tails for a rabbeted joint (center), the work is clamped in the jig as if routing a flush joint. But a scrap is clamped in the top position to back up the cut.

To reach beyond the rabbet and get a socket deep enough to accommodate the tail (right), the front must be shifted forward in the jig. The amount you shift it equals the width of the rabbet. A scrap, rabbeted appropriately, is clamped in place of the side to position the front.

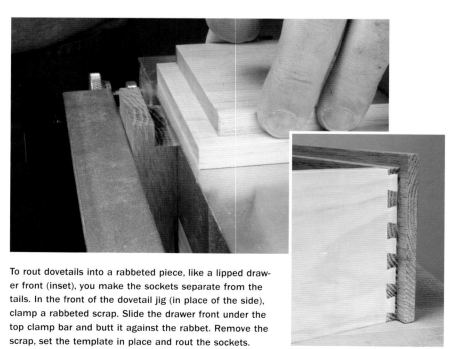

To rout dovetails into a rabbeted piece, like a lipped drawer front (inset), you make the sockets separate from the tails. In the front of the dovetail jig (in place of the side), clamp a rabbeted scrap. Slide the drawer front under the top clamp bar and butt it against the rabbet. Remove the scrap, set the template in place and rout the sockets.

Hand-Cut Half-Blinds

Have you hand-cut through dovetails? You'll have little trouble doing half-blinds, even though they are usually considered more difficult than through dovetails. And if you haven't hand-cut any dovetails, this is a tougher starting point. But you can do it.

The chief difficulty with half-blinds is cutting the sockets in the ends of the drawer front. The saw-cuts that establish the margins of the pins can't penetrate to the socket bottom — you don't want to cut through the front face. In addition, you're limited to chiseling from the inner face, again because you don't want to cut into the front face.

The techniques and tricks described in cutting through dovetails apply to cutting half-blinds too. You can start with the pins or the tails. You can use guide blocks to support and guide your saw, and to support and guide your chisel. But the work then becomes awfully fussy and time consuming.

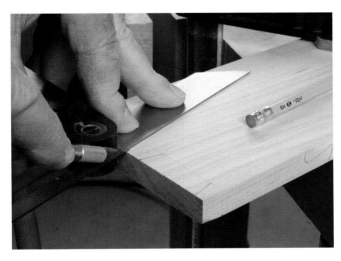

After scribing the baseline on the tail board's faces and edges with marking gauge, lay out tails. Clamp the board flat on the bench, overhanging the edge. Set a bevel gauge to the angle of dovetail you want. With the gauge handle against the board's end, scribe lines from the baseline to the end.

Secure the board in the vise so you can extend the layout lines across the end grain. Use a small square and the marking knife to score the wood.

Saw down to the baseline on the waste side of the layout lines. Use guide blocks if they help you keep the saw aligned.

Chop out the waste, beginning at baseline. Complete chopping the tails from the other side of the board.

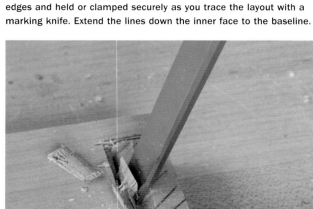

After scribing the baseline and depth lines on the drawer front with a marking gauge, transfer tail layouts with a marking knife. The tail board must be lined up perfectly with the depth line and the front's edges and held or clamped securely as you trace the layout with a marking knife. Extend the lines down the inner face to the baseline.

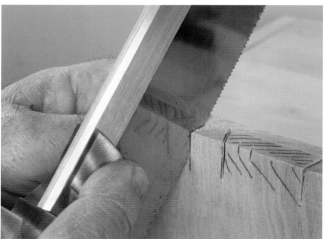

Clamp the drawer front in the vise at an angle that allows you to see both scribed lines. Saw to the waste side of the layout lines. Stop just shy of the lines.

Begin chopping out the pins, using the technique outlined in "Hand-cutting through Dovetails". Set the chisel just outside the baseline, hold it straight up and rap it with your mallet. After a starting blow at each waste site, lift a chip at each spot, then continue to deepen the cuts.

With half-blinds, it's practical to chop into the end grain to lift out the waste. You can't flip the board over and attack it from the front! Paring all the surfaces of the sockets is challenging. Skew chisels are helpful when digging waste out of corners.

Test the joint's fit. Use some judgment in the fitting. Repeatedly seating the joint, then knocking it apart crushes the wood fibers and can actually degrade the fit. Many experienced craftsmen check the fit without completely seating the joint, and save that for the final glueup.

A Power Assist

The ornery part of hand-cutting half-blind dovetails is chopping out those sockets for the tails. You can save yourself a lot of work by roughing out the sockets with a router. You can use any router, but a small one, like a laminate trimmer, is ideal. Routing with a straight bit is good, but a dovetail bit is even better, since it shapes the pins.

You want a vertical surface at the back of the socket, so you must stop the cut when the tips of the dovetail bit are aligned with the baseline. (At the surface, of course, this stops the cut short of the baseline.) To determine where to plant a fence, add the radius of the bit to the radius of the router base. In the photos, I'm using a trimmer with a $3^1/2$"-diameter base (radius $1^3/4$") and a $1/2$"bit (radius $1/4$"). Add the two dimensions, measure that distance (2") from the end of the pin board and locate the stop fence there.

Make the cuts free-hand. You may choose to deliberately stay to the waste side of the lines, but with practice, you'll find it easy to rout very close.

I've found it helpful to clamp the work to an elevated work surface and to sit on a stool. This makes it easier to see what the router is cutting. Wear goggles.

When making half-blinds, it's easier to transfer a tail layout to the pin board than the other way around. With the pin board in the vise, align the tail board with the scribed baseline. Knife along each tail.

Set the router with an appropriate dovetail bit in it on the inner face of the pin board. Adjust the bit to align with the baseline.

LEFT Here's my makeshift workstation — a wooden box clamped to the bench. The purpose is to elevate the work so I can see the end of the drawer front as I rout. To the box, I clamp the front, and atop that a fence to limit how far in the router can cut.

ABOVE Guide the trimmer freehand. I grip the motor barrel with one hand and guide the base with the other. Find an approach that you are comfortable with.

When the routing is done, the slope of the pin walls is established, as is the depth and length of the socket. The back wall must be chiseled to a vertical, and the pins pared to the lines.

Chopping the end wall vertical is the biggest part of cleanup left. Align the chisel in the baseline and strike it sharply with the mallet. Then chop into the waste horizontally to lift out the chip. After the end is clean, pare the margins of the pins.

CHAPTER FIVE

Building and Fitting Your Drawer

It's not enough to know how drawers are constructed. You've got to be able to actually build one. Of course you have to be able to fit it properly. Will it jam or rattle? And what will you do in either case?

You select a style, and the joinery and materials. You build the housing and ready the drawer pocket. The goal is a strong drawer that opens and closes easily and quietly, no shimmying or chattering, neither looseness nor sticking.

The approaches (and results) vary widely.

Some are perfunctory. They take a few measurements and write them down. They cut the parts to the written-down dimensions, zip through the joinery cuts, and knock the drawer together. Does it fit? Sometimes yes, sometimes no.

Others are persnickety. Every detail is sweated. "The fitted solid-wood drawer is a luxury for your finest work," says noted craftsman and teacher Ian Kirby. "A drawer like this is not a casual undertaking. It's neither quick nor easy — nor is it cheap. You have to allow about a day of bench work per drawer. It's too rich for many applications."

The happy medium is mastered, I think, by challenging yourself to make and fit a luxurious drawer or two. To grow as a woodworker, to improve the quality of your work and the ease and speed with which you do it, you need to eschew the perfunctory. But watch out for persnickety!

Making Fronts

A drawer front can be an integral part of the drawer, or just a façade that's stuck on an otherwise generic box.

Nine times out of ten, "making the front" is a matter of choosing a piece of wood. It's an important decision because the front is the part of the drawer that's on display. Yet it often comes down to ripping and cross-cutting a piece of the primary stock to fit. It becomes an economic rather than aesthetic judgment: "I've got this short that will fit. I don't want to start another board."

The real craftsman addresses the issue up front, before cutting any wood for a project. He or she will set out the available boards and look for harmony in figure and color. If the piece has several drawers in a row, the common practice is to cut them from one board and use them in "board order," so the figure flows across the piece. Yes, it is often very subtle.

But seldom do you want the converse: A jarring mishmash of color and figure. Drawer fronts with obvious glue-lines across them. A chest of drawers that's a patchwork of hues and textures may be a conscious choice, but all too often it's an unintended consequence of a casual, thoughtless manner of working in the shop.

So begin your drawer making with your mind in an artistic set. Lay out the drawer fronts so they put on a good show. And as you cut the boards and dress them, be sure you mark each one so you don't — while toiling in your workman's mindset — bollix your visual plan.

Having cut a board into multiple drawer fronts, be sure to label each piece so you "reassemble" the board in the correct sequence as you make and fit the drawers to the pockets. I mark the order and indicate which edge is the top.

The end result is low-key, subtle. But making drawer fronts involves more than exercising good mechanical skills, cutting the wood square, planing it true, fitting everything to close, uniform tolerances. It begins with the selection of the wood, so adjacent fronts harmonize with each other and with the case that houses them.

Be aesthetically judgmental in laying out drawer fronts. Plane your stock to expose the figure, texture and color of the wood. Try to use individual wide boards for wide (tall) fronts, rather than gluing up narrow ones. If two or more fronts will be side by side, take all from a single board, and keep them in "board order." If two or more rows of drawers are involved, set out the stock for all the rows as you mark them for crosscutting.

Curved Fronts

Making a curved drawer front involves more than choosing a piece of wood. Sometimes a lot more. But curved forms are pleasing and have been used in furniture for centuries. The end product makes the effort worthwhile.

The least involved way to make a curved drawer front is to cut it from a big block of solid wood. The expense for the material is high, and the resulting front tends to be coarse-looking. In terms of structural integrity, the solid-wood front ought to be limited to mild curved. Otherwise, the end grain is too weak to support sound joints.

An alternative is to bend veneers over a form, gluing them face-to-face. In some cases, you can use an inexpensive wood for the core veneers and save the best stock for the face veneers.

Other alternatives — various approaches to stack lamination — are easier than bent lamination but generally require you to veneer the face and edges to conceal the core.

These concave drawer fronts are bent laminations. Designer/builder Ken Burton resawed walnut into veneers, then laminated them between forms, much as outlined on pages 128-131.

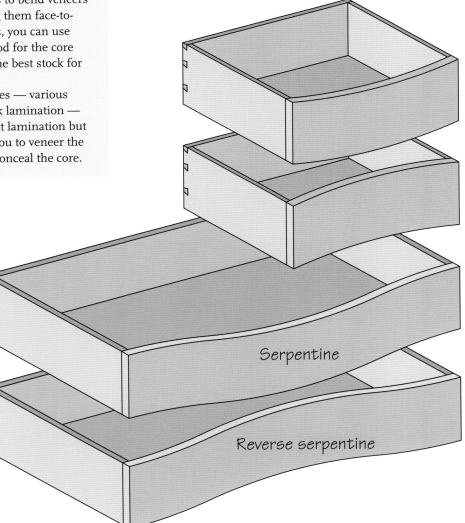

Serpentine

Reverse serpentine

Bandsawing a Curved Front

The most straightforward method of making a curved drawer front is to cut it from solid stock on the band saw. You begin with a block of 8/4 or even 12/4 stock, depending on the size of the front and the radius of the curve.

Join and plane the faces and edge of the blank. Lay out the curve on its edge. You have to saw the first face freehand — without a fence, following the layout line. Clean the saw marks from this face before cutting the second face. If you're bold (or perhaps foolhardy), you can use a belt sander. But a sharp spokeshave smooths the surface with less risk, noise and fine dust.

Set a marking gauge to the desired final thickness and, guided by the smoothed curved face, lay out a parallel curved line.

Use a point fence when you saw the second face. A point fence is a piece of wood, one end chamfered to a point, set on edge on the band saw table, with the point adjacent to the blade's teeth. The gap between the point and the blade matches the thickness of the front. The point guides the stock and allows you to pivot the stock to follow the line.

Set the smooth, curved face against the point and begin sawing. Hold the stock firmly against the fence as you saw, pivoting the stock to follow the line. Feed the work slowly, because overfeeding can cause the blade to deflect.

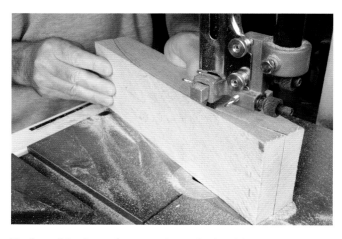

The face of the drawer front must be cut freehand. Lay out the curve you want on the stock's top edge, and saw carefully to the line.

Smooth the sawed face with a spokeshave or a belt sander. You want to remove the band saw marks and establish an even, fair curve.

Set a marking gauge to the thickness of the drawer front and scribe the second face parallel to the first.

Saw the second face using a point fence as a guide. Hold the work firmly to the fence and pivot it to follow the layout line.

Stack Laminations

Cutting curved drawer fronts from solid wood wastes high-priced lumber. The resulting drawer front isn't always as refined and attractive as you might expect. Though it's more laborious, creating a core of the desired shape and applying veneer to it ofttimes is the better approach.

Several ways to make the core — all of which can be called stack laminations — present themselves.

The most straightforward is to dress strips of a secondary stock and laminate them face to face, forming a major block of wood. Consider it a single, solid piece and cut the contour on the band saw.

A more elaborate approach is to brick-lay the stack. You crosscut your stock into little bricks, mitering the ends in the process. Then glue the bricks together, end-to-end and face-to-face, forming a roughly curved stack.

Glue cured, you saw the contour you want on the band saw.

The third stack lamination method is ideal for the woodworker who's not entirely comfortable band-sawing a smooth, even curve from a very thick block of wood. You saw curved pieces from 4/4 or 5/4 stock. Those you build up into your stack lamination, one strip at a time. The first strip you template-rout to match the layout pattern. As each strip is glued to the stack, you template-rout it to match the previous one.

A benefit of stack laminations is that they create a more stable face for your drawer front. You remember, no doubt, that radial movement is always less than tangential movement. By stacking plain-sawed stock face-to-face, you're creating a face that's all edge grain; in the stack-lam drawer front, the tangential movement is in the thickness, while the radial movement is in the height.

Make a pattern of ¹/₄" or ¹/₂" MDF. You use it to lay out all the staves needed to build up the desired drawer-front height. You also use it as template to shape the first rough-sawed stave on the router table.

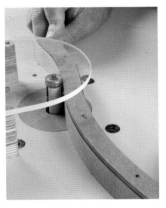

Bond a stave to the template with carpet tape. Use a flush-trimming bit — one with the pilot bearing on its tip — in a table-mounted router to smooth the stave and duplicate the template.

Sawing a strip with an undulating contour from a 1"-thick board is less daunting than sawing that contour in a 6"- or 8"-thick block. Stay outside the pencil lines, but don't worry too much about making each strip identical to each other.

After separating the template from the routed stave, glue and clamp a rough-cut stave to it. Be sure the rough stave's edges are proud of the smooth one's edges all around.

Rout the rough stave to match the smooth one using the same router-table setup you used to shape the first stave. When you're done, glue another stave to the core, then rout it to match. You build up the drawer front, one layer at a time.

Bent Lamination

This technique involves resawing lumber into thin veneers (1/16" to 3/32" thick), then gluing them back together. The stack of veneers are bent over a form and clamped there until the glue sets. Each drawer front is formed of 8 to 12 layers (or plies) of the veneer.

You can buy veneers for the job, or you can resaw your own. Resawing is covered in chapter 3: Choosing Materials. The entire lamination can be primary-wood veneers. Or you can sandwich secondary-wood veneers between two leaves of the primary wood.

A good way to glue-laminate the veneers into a curved drawer-front blank, one that doesn't require special-purpose equipment, uses two forms, a convex one and a concave one. The plies to be laminated are placed between these forms, and then the forms are clamped together, forcing the plies into the curved contour.

The laminating process itself doesn't take a great deal of time, but it does take hours for the glue to set. As a practical matter, you'll be able to do one drawer front a day.

Templating the Curve

Construction begins with a curve, the curve you want the drawer front to have. You make a template of the curve and use it in shaping the drawer dividers and in making the plies for the bending forms.

Cut a template blank from 1/4" hardboard or MDF, cutting the blank 4" wider than the form plies ultimately will be. The extra length will make routing easier and safer. Lay out the curve and cut to the line using a band saw or a jigsaw. Smooth the curve with a cabinetmaker's rasp, file or coarse sandpaper. Label this template the master.

Make the working templates, one convex, the other concave, next. Cut a single piece of 1/4" material large enough to produce the two templates. Stick the master to this blank. Cut with a pattern bit or flush-trim bit, feeding the master's edge along the bit's pilot bearing, forming a duplicate of the master and a complementary template with one cut.

Glue fences to both templates to trap the work.

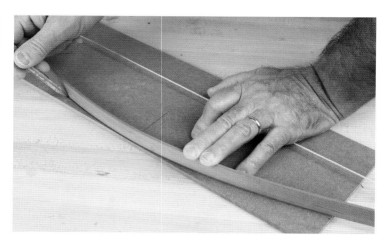

Lay out the crest and the end points of the curve on the template blank, then lay out the curve. An easy way to produce a curve is to flex a thin ripping so it is aligned with each of the three marks.

After sawing to the line, fair the curve with a cabinetmaker's rasp. Hold the rasp at an angle and work it in line with the curve, taking down high spots and eliminating flat spots.

Make the working templates by cutting through a 1/4" blank with a flush-trim bit guided by the master template. The diameter of the bit should match the thickness of the lamination you are going to make. The master template should overhang the blank so you can engage the bearing before the cutting edges contact the workpiece.

Constructing the Forms

Each form is built up of multiple plies cut from MDF or particleboard. The height of the widest drawer front dictates how many plies are needed. You cut a stack of blanks from sheet stock, and shape an edge of each blank using one template or the other. Glue and screw these plies face-to-face. The edges form a broad surface with the contour you want for the drawer front.

Cut the blanks for the plies, sizing each so it yields both a concave and a convex ply.

Fit one of your two templates on an MDF blank and fasten them together with 1 or 2 screws. With a jigsaw or on the band saw, cut the MDF close to the template. (Save the cut-off piece of the blank to be shaped with the other template.) At the router table, use a straight pattern bit, which has a shank-mounted pilot bearing, to rout the MDF to match template's curve. Cut all the pieces needed for the two forms in this way.

Glue and screw the plies together. Spread glue on the first piece, and lay another ply on top of it. Register them by aligning the edges flush. Run 2 or 3 screws through this ply into the previous one. Then spread glue on the surface and add another ply, squaring the edges and screwing it in place. Build up the form in this way.

Before putting the forms to use, wax them heavily. The wax makes it easier to clean off glue and should prevent the lamination from bonding to the form.

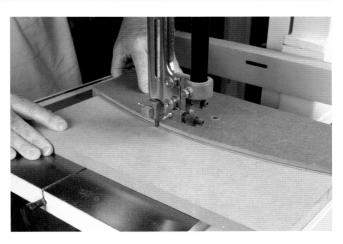

LEFT Fit one of your working templates onto a blank, which should be big enough to yield a ply for the convex form and one for the matching concave form. The template's fences should register the template tightly on the blank. Drill through the template into the blank and drive a screw to fasten the two together.

At the band saw, cut the blank close to the guiding edge of the template. Set the cut-off piece aside to be shaped with the other working template.

RIGHT At the router table, shape the blank to perfectly match the template's contour. Use a straight pattern bit. Routing MDF and particleboard produces clouds of fine dust; be sure you have first-rate dust collection when you do this job.

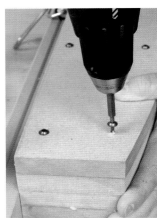

Building up each form layer by layer. A fence clamped to the bench top helps align the plies. Squirt glue onto the surface of a ply and spread it with a printmaker's brayer, a hard rubber roller available at art supplies outlets (LEFT). Set a fresh ply on top of the glue-coated one and drive screws to hold them together while the glue sets (RIGHT).

Laminating the Drawer Fronts

Drawer fronts range in thickness from ⁵⁄₈" up to ⁷⁄₈", seldom more than that. If your veneers are about ¹⁄₁₆" thick, you need 9 plies for a ⁵⁄₈" thickness, and as many as 12 plies for a ³⁄₄" thickness. If you use thicker plies, then you'd need fewer to achieve the drawer-front thickness you want.

To give the appearance of a solid board in the finished lamination, glue the veneers together in the order that they came off the saw. This helps conceal glue lines and gives a more natural look to the work.

It's essential to work quickly during a glue-up. You must have the forms at hand, well waxed and ready for the laminate bundle. Your clamps also must be ready. Set a pair of horses beside the workbench, and rest the concave form across them so you'll have unobstructed access to all sides with the clamps.

Lay out the veneers. Stack them in the order you want them in the glue-up, and work out a routine for keeping them in that order and orientation as you spread the glue.

Choose a glue. Some woodworkers prefer epoxy or plastic resin (urea formaldehyde) glue for laminations. Both have long working times so you won't risk having the glue set before you've got all the plies stacked, bent over the form and clamped. Just as important, epoxy and plastic resin glues are more creep-resistant than yellow glue. (Creep is the tendency of the individual plies in a lamination to move slightly, making the edge of the work feel rough to the touch. In a worst-case situation, creep can alter the contour of a lamination.)

Nevertheless, I count myself among the yellow polyvinyl acetate users, even for glue-laminations. It's readily available and cheap, already mixed, non-toxic and easy to clean up. Yes, it sets quickly, but for the drawer-front laminations I've done, that's never been a problem. And, slow-set varieties are available. Likewise, creep hasn't been evident.

When you are ready to go, apply glue to the mating surfaces of the veneers. A print-makers brayer is a great tool for this. It's like a small paint roller, but its hard rubber roller makes it easy to keep the glue spread thin. You need to expect beads of glue to squeeze out of the seams as you apply the clamps. But rivers of glue welling from the seams indicate you used way too much glue. It's a nightmare to clean up.

Spreading glue on the veneers doesn't have to be a messy job. I do the job on a scrap of melamine, so the glue doesn't get all over the bench top. Squirt glue onto the veneer and spread it uniformly across the surface with a printmaker's brayer, which is like a hard-rubber paint roller.

Set the veneer on the stack resting on the form with its glue-covered surface up. Work the new ply back and forth to tack it to the glue on the previous piece.

Clamping the two forms to bend the veneers isn't much different than clamping a panel. Begin by applying and tightening a pair of clamps at the center. Get them just as tight as you can. Then add however many other clamps you can.

With the leaf of veneer on the bench top, spread glue on the first face. The first piece goes on the form with the glue-side up. All subsequent ones are set onto the stack on the form, glue-side down. After you place a leaf on the stack, spread glue on its uncoated face. The last piece set on the stack doesn't get a glue application on its exposed face, of course.

Set the convex form on top of the stack and apply the clamps. Work as quickly as possible. You might picture the plies slippin' and slidin' and the wood resisting being bent, but that's not the way it works in practice. If you use yellow glue, its tack will keep the individual plies from slithering far out of alignment. And there isn't much resistance to the bending.

Apply clamps, starting at the center and working toward the ends. The amount of movement needed to pull the laminates to the form is small, well within the range of even pipe clamps.

Allow the glue time to set fully. Plan on leaving the drawer front in the form 8 to 12 hours. If you do one front a day, you can give the glue nearly 24 hours to set.

After the glue has set, free the drawer front from the forms. Set it aside until you are ready to make the drawers. Clean any dried glue from the forms, rewax them, and do another lamination.

Allow a glue-laminated drawer front several days to cure and stabilize. Clean up an edge with a scraper, then joint it. Brace the convex face against the fence and feed the piece in an arc across the cutterhead. You want the edge straight; getting it square to the face is less of a concern at this point.

Rip the front to width in two passes. Keep the convex face down on the saw table as you cut. Clean up the unjointed edge first, straightening the edge and squaring it to the face. Then skim the jointed edge to square it and bring the piece to width. A slow but constant feed rate yields best results.

Crosscutting the front is next. The cuts must trim the ends parallel to the run of the drawer. Stand the front on edge against the template you used to shape the lamination form plies. Mark at the trap fences on the front's inner face, then extend the line with a square.

Trim the ends of the drawer fronts with a crosscut sled on the table saw. Rest the front in a simple cradle for the cuts. Make sure the cut will be parallel to the layout line before cutting to the line.

Fit the Parts

The craftsman has at least two goals when fitting a drawer to its pocket.

First is a smooth, even operation — a wooden drawer that just glides open and closed. You want the drawer to open easily and quietly. No sticking, no chattering, no jiggling or wiggling from side to side. You want it to close the same way. No jamming, but no rattling either. You'd like to feel just a bit of resistance, a rush of air being forced out of the pocket.

You want that fabled "piston fit."

The second goal is visual: A front that floats in its "frame" with a consistent gap all around. This is especially true when the drawer front is flush to the front edge of the cabinet. It helps to have a perfectly square pocket to work with, of course. But the proof of a woodworker's skill is how he or she fits a drawer front to a slightly skewed pocket.

There are those who'll tell you it's easy. And after you've done it a few times, it does get easier. The trick is to fit the individual parts to the pocket before you cut the joinery and assemble the drawer. You have to take your time to get it right.

Front

Start with the drawer front. Rip and crosscut the drawer front about 1/8" over-wide and similarly over-long.

Check the drawer pocket to assess whether the drawer divider is flat and square to the sides, and so on. Plane an edge of the front to match the drawer divider. Next, plane, sand, or trim the right end of the front to match the case side. Fit the left end. Finally, plane the top edge.

When you are done, the drawer front should fit so snugly that it can be pushed in just halfway.

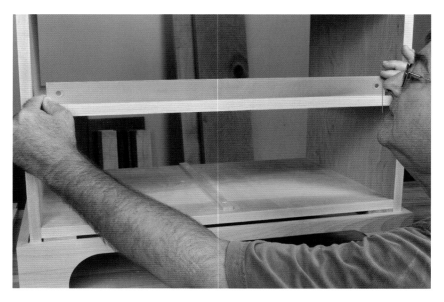

The first edge you address when fitting the drawer front is the bottom one. Check the divider with a straightedge to see if it is straight.

Plane the bottom edge of the front to smooth it. If the divider is crowned or sagging, plane a matching contour into that edge.

Check the angle between the divider and the case side. If it's not perfectly square, capture the angle with a sliding bevel.

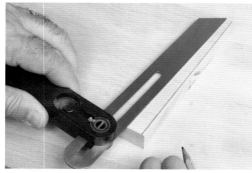

Transfer the angle to the appropriate end of the front. Of course, the front needs to be long enough to allow minor trimming in such situations.

Use a sharp bench plane — not a little block plane — to trim the front's end to match the pencil line. You can also use a belt sander (right) to accomplish the work, but be careful! It is way too easy to scrub off too much material, or to sand a bevel or a hollow into the edge without realizing it.

Address the opposite end of the drawer front next. Catch the just-trimmed end in the case and mark along the opposite case side on the front's top edge (left). Reposition the front so you can mark the bottom edge too (right). Use a marking knife for the most accurate measure. Draw a line between the two knife-marks and plane the end to the line.

Check the front's fit in the opening. Plane the top edge as necessary to allow it to fit partway into place. At this stage, you don't really want it to fit easily into the opening; it should be very snug.

Sides and Back

Fit the sides to the case. Measure and rip the side stock just a hair over-width. Then one side at a time, plane the piece until it just slides in snugly. Crosscut the back end square. Determine how far into the case you want it to go, account for the joinery, and crosscut the front end, squaring it.

If you're like me, you don't want the drawer to extend all the way to the case back. The clunk you hear when the drawer hits the back isn't the sound of fine crafts-manship. Equally bad is the impact it has on fit. When solid-wood case sides shrink, the drawer stands just a bit proud on the case's front edges. When those sides shrink, the drawer may slide in just a bit too far.

It's better to make the drawers a fraction of an inch shorter than the case depth and mount closing stops on the drawer dividers.

Assuming you are joining the back to the sides with through dovetails, the drawer back fits the opening from side to side. Some craftsmen advocate crosscutting the back $1/16$" shorter than the front to make final fitting easier. If some joinery other than through dovetails will be used, the length of the back has to be adjusted.

Typically, the back rests on the drawer bottom and is flush with the top edges of the sides. So you'd subtract something like $1/2$" from the drawer side width — $1/4$" bottom-groove width plus $1/4$" groove offset from the side's bottom edge — to determine the back's width.

Rest the bottom corner of a roughly-sized drawer side on the lower divider and mark where it contacts the upper divider. Rip the side to that mark.

Check the fit of the side in the drawer pocket. It should glide in and out without binding, but it shouldn't have top to bottom play. If the fit is too snug, take a shaving or two off the edge with a hand plane.

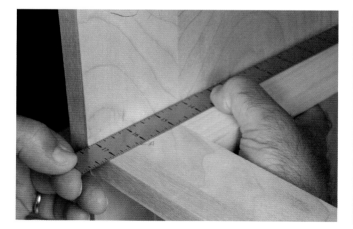

Measure the case depth. From that subtract the amount the front will overlap the side (about $1/4$" if you're using half-blind dovetails, for example) and the space you want between the drawer and the case back.

To determine the height of the back, measure the side from the bottom groove to the top edge.

Cut the Joinery

With the parts cut and fitted to their drawer pocket, cut the joinery. Front to sides, back to sides and bottom to drawer box. I've already outlined how to cut many joints commonly used for drawers. So the point here is not how to cut the joinery, but how to fit it. You don't want the snug fit you are aiming for to be lost because of the way the joinery is cut and fitted.

From the standpoint of fit, you should cut the joint, whatever it is, ever-so-slightly under-depth so the side stands proud of the end of the front. The offset of the side in relation to the front's end should be tiny; $1/64"$ is plenty.

What this does is preserve the fit you've established of front to drawer pocket. After you've glued up the drawer, it probably won't fit the pocket. As we'll see, tweaking the drawer's fit involves planing or sanding the sides. First you get them flush with the ends of the front, and then you take the entire surface down shaving by shaving until it fits the drawer pocket perfectly.

An oft-suggested alternative is to cut the joint slightly over-depth, on the notion that it's easier to plane or sand the end of the front flush with the side, rather than the other way around. The shortcoming is seen from the standpoint of fit. You sacrifice the snug fit of the front in the drawer-pocket opening that you already invested time and effort to achieve.

In pursuing the grail of fit, you have to assume extra burdens and endure some additional work. The work isn't difficult, but you won't find shortcuts.

It's not just for dovetails. Regardless of the joinery you use, cut it so the side is slightly proud of the front's end.

Sand the inner faces of the drawer parts before cutting the joinery. Doing it afterwards may affect how the joints fit. This is especially true of dovetails.

Tails slightly proud of the pins is the fit you want in a drawer joint. Yes, it's a bit more work to plane down the side so it's flush with the drawer front's end. But that preserves the snug fit of the front to the drawer pocket.

Bottom Groove

After cutting the sides-to-front and sides-to-back joinery, plow the bottom groove.

Typically, the groove is located so the underside of the drawer bottom is about $5/16$" from the bottom edge of the drawer box. This placement offers clearance for closing stops on the drawer divider.

However, undermount mechanical slides probably require the bottom to be $1/2$" from the edges of the drawer box. Confirm the necessary clearance before grooving.

Which parts need grooves depend on the drawer design. If you're using slips, only the front is grooved. If the bottom is fully enclosed, the back must be grooved as well as the front and sides.

Assuming you use $1/4$" plywood for the bottom, the groove should be less than $1/4$" wide or else the bottom will rattle. Groove depth depends on the thickness of the drawer-side stock.

You can cut through-grooves quickly and easily. At the table saw, a first pass establishes the bottom shoulder of the groove, while a second pass widens the groove just enough to produce a snug fit. A single pass on the router table — try using a $7/32$" straight bit or slot cutter — will do the job too.

Stopped grooves are more troublesome; cut them on the router table. A stopped groove is occasionally necessary to avoid groove exposure to the front or the sides of a drawer. Think of a drawer assembled with box joints.

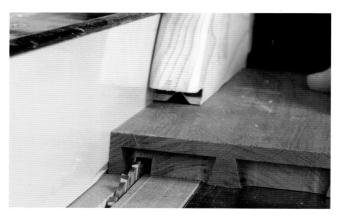

Sawing the typical bottom groove is fast and trouble-free. Set the blade height, position the rip fence, and cut all the workpieces. After adjusting the fence away from the blade to widen the groove, make a second and final pass on all the pieces.

Stopped grooves are best done on the router table with a straight bit. Use stop blocks to position the work for the beginning of the groove and to arrest the feed at the cut's terminus. You've got to plunge the work onto the bit to begin the cut, and tip it up off the bit to end the cut.

Cutting a bottom groove in a curved drawer front is best done on the router table with a slot cutter. Use the correct diameter of pilot bearing to limit the groove's depth. Use a starting pin to control the workpiece at the beginning of the cut, and slide the work in an arc through the cut.

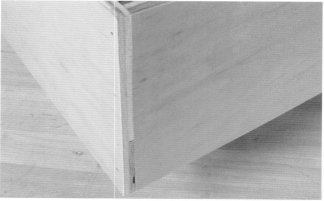

Bottom grooves are barely concealed in drawers banged out for most kitchen cabinetry. You plow through grooves in sides, back, and structural front by whatever means is fastest. The tell-tale notch is out of sight at the back and covered by an applied front.

Glued-Up

The assembly process varies with the joinery and the size of the drawer. In every case, careful assembly is essential. Do the job on a flat surface. Be sure the drawer sets flat and is square.

Drawers joined with dovetails seldom need to be clamped, though seating the joints by momentarily clamping them ("nip them home," as Ian Kirby puts it) is often beneficial. Some craftsmen don't even like to dry assemble dovetails. If the dovetails are as tight as they should be, the thinking goes, then testing them will compress the wood fibers and the joint will be too loose later.

Be judicious in your use of glue. An over-application will squeeze out and make a mess. Just spread a little bit of glue on the long grain of the pins and perhaps a bit at front edge of the tails. Use a thin stick or small brush as an applicator. Tap the joint closed with a dead blow mallet or force it home with a clamp. Make sure the drawer is flat, not twisted in the slightest, and check it for square. Then leave the drawer unclamped while the glue sets.

Many joints other than dovetails are used in assembling drawers, and just about all of them do require clamping. Your aim is to have a drawer that looks good and performs well. So you need to assemble it with the same care you invested in fitting the parts and cutting the joints.

ABOVE Use a thin stick or small brush as an applicator. Apply a little bit of glue on the long grain of the pins and at front edge of the tails.

LEFT Apply a clamp — perhaps two or three to a tall drawer — to seat the dovetails. If the dovetails are properly fitted, the clamping only needs to be momentary; just tight enough to seat the joint. Remove the clamp(s) and check the alignment of the drawer.

BELOW As soon as the dovetails are seated and the clamps removed, check the drawer to ensure it is square and flat. Sight across the top edges of the drawer for indications of twist. Compare the diagonal measurements to confirm that the box is square.

Not all joinery is self-aligning. Assemble the drawer dry — without glue — so you can determine how many clamps you'll need and get them ready. Work on a flat surface.

Apply clamps in a sequence that will seat the joints, pulling the front and back against the ends of the sides, then the sides against the shoulders of the joints.

Make sure the drawer is flat. Squat down and sight across the upper edges of the box, as if you were using winding sticks. The edges of the sides must be parallel.

Finally, measure the diagonals to ensure the box is square.

Slips

Make the slips as you are cutting drawer parts, but do the final fitting and glue them in place only after the drawer is glued up.

Recall that the slip's function is to allow the drawer sides to be thin, which looks better, and still have a wide edge for the drawer to slide on. Glued to the side's inner face, the slip stiffens it. In addition, it offers girth for the bottom groove.

In general, a slip is about ¹/₂" thick, and it extends, of course, just about the full length of the drawer side. The vertical dimension (the width) depends on the profile. A flush slip matches the distance from the side's bottom edge to the upper surface of the drawer bottom. A beveled or a beaded slip must be taller.

Rather than groove and profile a strip that probably measures ¹/₂" × ³/₄" — too slender to safely work with power tools — work the edges of a wider board, then rip the shaped slip from it.

Traditionally, the slip's front end is rabbeted across the top and bottom to form a short tenon that fits into the drawer front's bottom groove. Similarly, the tail end is rabbeted across the top surface to accommodate the drawer back and allow the slip to end flush with the back end of the drawer side.

To avoid damaging the profile, the sequence of cuts should be to groove the workpiece, then form the tenon, then rout the profile, and finally, rip the individual slip from the workpiece. Crosscut the slip to fit its drawer and rabbet the end.

ABOVE Slips can be strictly functional or modestly decorative, as exemplified by these samples.

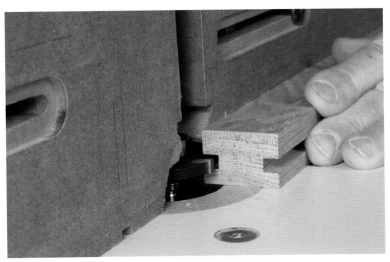

LEFT Make the slips in pairs, so you aren't working unnecessarily narrow strips. After ripping and crosscutting the blanks to size, cut the bottom groove in both edges.

Form a small tenon on the front end of the slip blank by rabbeting across both the top and bottom surfaces. Use the same cutter, but adjust the height so the tenon aligns perfectly with the groove.

A profile, if there is to be one, is routed next, adjacent to the groove. Rout a bevel, a cove (as here), a quarteround, even an ogee, doing the job on the router table.

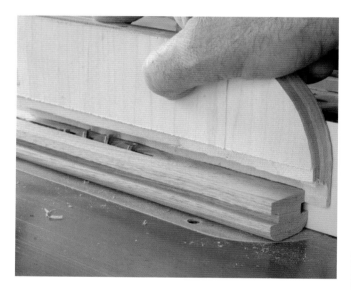

Rip the slips from the blank. Smooth the just-cut surface for gluing to the drawer side with a swipe with a hand plane.

ABOVE Fit each slip to the assembled drawer box. A profile must be trimmed to accommodate the back. Insert the tenon in the drawer front's bottom groove and mark across the tail end at the drawer back for trimming.

LEFT Glue the slip to the drawer side. Plane the bottom surface flush with the bottom edge of the side. Be wary of over-planing at this time; the drawer is yet to be fitted.

Tweaking the Fit

The glue has set, the clamps are off the drawer, and you are set to fit it into the case. If you're still with me, you may be feeling a pang or two of concern because ... well ... the drawer is just a wee bit too tight. You can only push it partway into its pocket. Maybe you can't even get it engaged in the opening: It's just too wide. Or too tall. Or both.

Oh, good. You *are* still with me. Because you've now got to tweak the fit. And if the drawer slides into place, chances are you won't achieve that snug, smooth-running fit you want. Fitting is a reductive process. You want to remove material from the edges and sides of the drawer.

Clean Up the Joints

The first step is to clean up the joints. Lightly plane the bottom edges of the drawer box. If the box has slips, make sure they are flush with the edges of the sides. Check across the width of the drawer with a straightedge to ensure that the edges are in the same plane.

Next plane (or sand) the dovetails (or other joinery) flush at the back of the drawer sides. How much you work these areas — beyond leveling the pins — depends upon whether or not the drawer fits into the pocket, and upon how far in it fits, and too, upon how easily it moves. The repeated test fittings needed to track your progress can legitimately be seen as tedious. That's how I view it, anyway. Tedious but necessary.

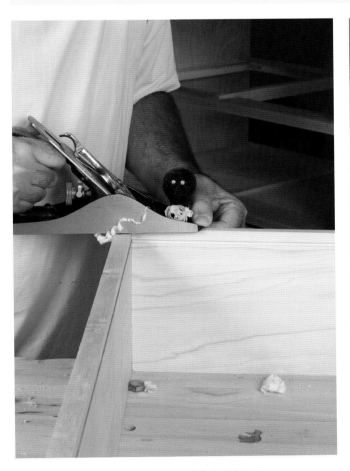

The first step in tweaking the drawer's fit is to lightly plane the bottom edges flush.

LEFT Sliding the drawer into its pocket to assess its fit. This drawer's side cupped slightly, so it won't enter the pocket at all. Planing or sanding at the back is needed.

BELOW Start at the back corners and plane the drawer sides. If the drawer is assembled with through dovetails at the back, plane the pins flush. Don't overdo it; interrupt your work frequently to check the drawer's fit in the case. The goal is a piston fit, and you've got to sneak up on it.

Shoot the Drawer

"Shooting the drawer," a term I picked up from Ian Kirby, means planing the sides down to the level of the dovetail pins. I'm ascribing to it the broader meaning of leveling the drawer side, so that regardless of what joinery you've used, the sides are flat and flush with the ends of the drawer front. And I'm embracing power sanding as well as hand planing to accomplish the work.

To hold the drawer, fit the front or back in your bench's vise and rest the side on a plank laid across the bench top (see photo).

Plane the drawer sides from end to end, first one side, then the other. Once you can slide the drawer all the way into its pocket, shift your attention to easing the movement. Slide the drawer in and out several times to burnish high spots where the drawer binds against case parts. Scrape or plane them.

Tailor your approach to the season. If you're making the drawer in the midst of winter, when humidity typically is low, make the fit a little loose. That way, the drawer will still work when the wood swells in the humidity of mid-summer.

Hand planing isn't the only means of removing material from drawer sides. A belt sander does the job just as well as a hand plane, and it may even be faster. But it is certainly noisier and dirtier.

LEFT AND BELOW To hold the drawer so you can plane or sand the side, grip its front or back in the vise and slide a plank resting on the bench top under the side. The plank needn't be clamped; that makes it easier to maneuver it into the drawer as you capture the drawer in the vise.

Plane the sides flush with the ends of the drawer front. Check the fit yet again, then work the ends of the drawer front until you have a consistent gap of about 1/32" at either end.

A drawer's pull is seldom mounted before it's fitted and finished. But while you're fitting the drawer to the case, you need to be able to open it. If the case doesn't have its back, you can push the drawer open. But sometimes you need a temporary pull, usually a single screw driven at the spot where the pull ultimately will be mounted.

Fit the Front

The drawer should slide in easily at this point. All that remains is to refine the gap around the drawer front. Planing the sides and drawer front until you achieve a $1/32$" gap at each end.

Examine the clearance at the top of the drawer. If necessary, plane the top edge to establish the same gap there.

Finally, relieve the bottom edge of the drawer front with a shoulder plane. Not only does this create an even gap all around the front, it prevents the drawer front from catching on the divider when it's pushed closed.

Keep checking the drawer's fit. When it comes within inches of closing fully, turn your attention to the front corners.

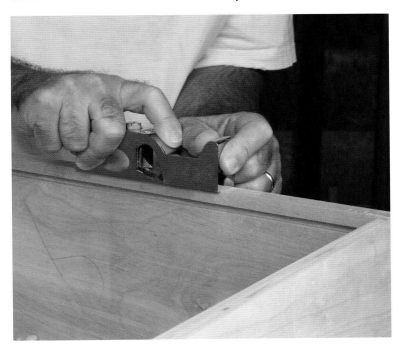

Finish up by planing the bottom edge of the drawer front to create the same gap between it and the drawer divider as you have at the top and the ends. Use a shoulder plane for this task.

A consistent gap around each drawer front is the goal. And you want to repeat the same gap around every front in the chest.

Installing the Bottom

When the drawer fits the case, cut and install the bottom. Measure the drawer itself, of course, to be sure the bottom you cut will fit. And be sure the bottom won't force the drawer out of the fit you've worked so hard to achieve. Plywood is by far the most common material used for drawer bottoms, and for good reason. It is strong, inexpensive, easy to cut and fit. It can be attractive (that depends on the face-veneer species). It can be easy to clean (particularly beneficial in a kitchen drawer). Solid wood is viable, though it does require a lot more work (see the next page).

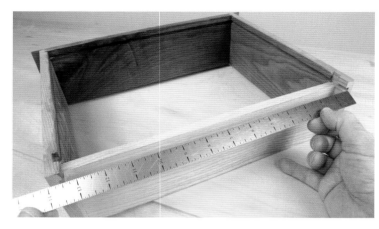

Cutting a bottom for a traditional open-back-construction drawer can wait until it's assembled. Use a rule (rather than a tape measure). Make sure you cut the bottom square (assuming the drawer itself is square), so sliding the bottom in doesn't skew it.

Grain orientation is critical with a solid-wood bottom (FAR LEFT), a minor aesthetic judgment with plywood (LEFT). A solid-wood bottom will expand and contract seasonally, and the wood must be oriented so it expands toward the back rather than side to side. Plywood is stable; the direction of the face veneer's grain can be oriented any which way.

Sheet goods suitable for drawer bottoms abound. Here are a few examples; all are $1/4$" thick. The drawer's use coupled with the appearance you want usually drive the choice.

1. Luan
2. Luan
3. Birch
4. Pre-finished birch
5. Cherry
6. Oak
7. MDF
8. Hardboard
9. MCP

Solid-wood Bottom

A solid-wood bottom is something that only the cognoscenti will recognize and appreciate. Its use requires a fair bit of extra work: Resawing stock, glue-ups, working the edges. But a solid-wood bottom is another subtle mark of the finest work.

The bottom can match the rest of the drawer's wood, and not only if you've used birch or maple for the secondary wood.

Though solid wood, the bottom need not be heavy and thick. Half-inch-thick stock is the upper end of the range to me. Depending on the drawer's dimensions, you can plane the wood down to $3/8"$, $5/16"$, even $1/4"$ and still have a sound, strong bottom.

Regardless of the drawer's dimensions and the species of wood you've chosen for the bottom, you should orient the grain to run from side to side. You want whatever wood movement that occurs to be front to back, rather than side to side. In the latter orientation, expansion of the bottom could distort the sides, degrading the fit and even breaking the drawer.

One result of the orientation is that you'll have to edge-glue thin stock to make short but wide panels. They generally won't be panels you can run through a lunch-box-size planer to level after glue-up. A couple of tactics to align the boards during glue-up are shown.

There's no reason why you can't house a solid-wood bottom in grooves in the drawer sides, but most often, the bottom is mated to slips. In any case, you will need to reduce the thickness of the panel's edges so they'll fit the grooves. The traditional method is to bevel the underside on three edges — not the back. Rabbeting or coving the edges also works, and in some applications is more appropriate.

Thin stock tends to be less stable than its thicker kin, so you can't make a drawer bottom, then let it lay around for days and days. If you can't put it into a drawer right away, sticker it and put some weight on it.

ABOVE LEFT **Make drawer bottoms from eastern red cedar, often known as aromatic cedar. You'll get the pleasant cedar scent without bulking up the drawer by lining it.**

ABOVE RIGHT **Clamps made from wood scraps, all-thread and nuts and washers trap a panel between two rods, which helps keep the panel from bowing when pressure is applied.**

LEFT **Aligning edge joints so the faces of adjacent boards are flush can be frustrating. You can get perfect alignment if you mill the stock's edges with the junior-size glue joint bit. The interlocking profile prevents boards from squirming out of alignment as you apply clamping pressure.**

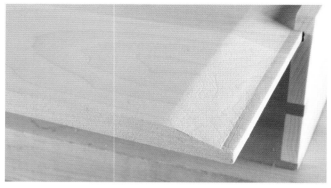

The edges of a solid-wood bottom can be beveled with a hand plane or on the table saw, but using a small panel-raising bit produces a flat tongue (right) that fits perfectly into grooves in the drawer box.

Coving the bottom edges of the panel with a roundnose bit is fast and yields an attractive appearance.

In a drawer with flush slips or with a muntin, rabbeting the top edges of the bottom panel produces a drawer bottom that's flush from one side to the other.

Secure the bottom to the drawer back with a washer-head screw driven through a slot cut in from the back edge of the bottom.

Muntins

A large drawer —large in length and width — often prompts worries about the drawer bottom. Will the conventional construction — 1/4" plywood bottom housed in grooves in the sides and front — be adequate? Will the bottom sag too much?

A good solution is a muntin. This frame piece stretches between the front and back, dividing the bottom opening of the drawer box in two. You use two smaller panels for the bottom. The whole drawer is reinforced and is stronger.

You make the muntin exactly the way you make a pair of slips, but you don't rip the grooved and profiled workpiece in two. A muntin should be about 1 1/4" to 2" wide.

The drawing on page 25 depicts a grooved-edge muntin that, inside the drawer, will be raised. If you want the bottom flat from side to side, you can rabbet the muntin instead of grooving it, or you can groove the muntin and rabbet the bottom panels. The rabbeted muntin is a good choice where the bottom panels are 1/4" plywood.

Need a strong drawer for storing your heavy metal? Reinforce the bottom using a muntin. The muntin divides the bottom into two sections and prevents worrisome sagging of a one-piece bottom. Depending on the bottom treatment (is it rabbeted or otherwise revealed at the top or bottom of the edges?), the muntin can be raised (TOP) or flush (ABOVE).

A stub tenon is the easiest way to join a muntin to a drawer front. Cut the tenon so it aligns with the grooves. Apply a bit of glue to it and plug it into the groove in the drawer front.

A stronger connection of muntin to drawer front is provided by a dovetail. Cut the tail on the muntin and transfer the shape to the drawer front with a marking knife.

Chop out the socket with chisel and mallet, or cut it with a dovetail bit in a small router. Apply glue to the tail and fit it into the socket.

However the muntin is attached to the drawer front, at the back it usually is fastened. Align it and drive a screw through it into the drawer back.

Finishing Up

The drawer is now all but done. What remains to be done, beyond installing pulls, is largely cosmetic — touching up gappy joints, easing edges and perhaps applying a finish.

Take a look at the joints first. Every woodworker crafts a gappy joint once in a while. It's not usually obvious when the joint is a rabbet or a lock joint, but, boy! do those little crevices or open seams pop out from dovetails and box joints.

Take heart! Cyanoacrylate glue (better known as super glue), is salve for the condition. The glue is made in several viscosities, and you want a thick mix. Squeeze it into the cracks you want to fill, and quickly rub in some sanding dust. Cyanoacrylate hardens in seconds, so you need to mix in the dust very quickly. Pause a couple of beats, then sand the surface.

You can repeat the process — and you may have to fill and level deeper crevices.

Ease the edges next. The goal simply is to take the sharpness off the edges, so they are more inviting to the touch. It isn't difficult or time-consuming. Wrap fine-grit sandpaper around a hardwood block and lightly sand the edges and corners, both inside and outside.

Fill narrow cracks in box joints or dovetails with cyanoacrylate glue and sanding dust. Squeeze a thick grade of the glue into the seams, then quickly force a sprinkling dust into it with fine-grit sandpaper.

Several applications of the glue and dust may be needed to obliterate the worst of the gaps.

If it's a crevice rather than a mere crack, a wedge may be the repair you need. Glue a small wedge into the gap. When the glue is dry, pare it flush with a chisel. Sand it smooth and no one will notice it.

With fine sandpaper wrapped around a hardwood block, lightly round the edges of the drawers. Be judicious: You want the edges to look sharp without being sharp.

Applying Finish

Most woodworkers know better than to apply an oil finish inside a drawer or case (it'll stink for years). Beyond that, however, they're less certain about finishing drawers. Many regard them as problematic to finish — and with some reason. Their inside corners, for example, seem to either resist finish or collect puddles of it.

Tage Frid advised against any finish except paraffin wax on the outsides of drawers and the insides of cases. "The finish will just gum up the works and might cause the drawer to stick."

But approach the job logically and you should have no difficulties.

First, decide which surfaces will be finished and which will not. Without doubt, the face, top edge and ends of the drawer front will be finished to match the rest of the piece. Whether you apply finish to the interior of a drawer, as well as what that finish might be, depend on the use of the drawer.

For clothing or linens, the less finish the better. Try a single coat of a 2 lb. cut of shellac. For a kitchen drawer or the like, a couple of coats of a tough film finish like polyurethane or lacquer are in order.

Next, tackle the job before you install the bottom and the pull. Without the bottom in place, it's far easier to get into those inside corners. Too, you can do a better job of finishing the bottom if it's separate. Having the pull mounted — even if it's wood and will be finished — or mounting holes drilled invite runs in the finish.

Finish the front first. If the primary wood is being stained, apply the stain first to the face and top edge of the drawer front. Use a fine artists brush (say a No.2 or No.4) to carefully apply stain to the ends of the front and around dovetail pins. While it's common to mask off the side and stain both pins and tails, that looks crummy. Take the time to do it right.

Apply the clear coat to the drawer front next. If you're using an oil finish on the piece of furniture, it may be difficult to use it on the drawer front and isolate it to the pins. One option suggested by finishing expert Jeff Jewitt is to apply it to the entire drawer side. After the oil finish is dry, apply a sealing coat of shellac to the drawer side.

Next finish the inside of the drawer, whether you use shellac, polyurethane or lacquer. An excellent applicator is a large artist's wash brush. Its sharp, chiseled edge gets into corners with aplomb. Let it dry a couple of hours, then lightly sand with 600-grit paper.

Apply paste wax to the drawer's interior, whether you've used a film finish or not. On sliding surfaces, use beeswax, a candle or paraffin (look for it with canning supplies at a supermarket).

The final job is to lay out and drill mounting holes for the pulls. Install the pulls and fit the drawers into their pockets.

Brush or pad shellac (or some other non-oil finish) on the inside of the drawer box before sliding the bottom in place. Finish the bottom separately.

Finish the drawer front first. Use whatever finish you are applying to the case.

To ease the drawer's action and prevent sticking, rub beeswax or paraffin wax on the drawer sides and bottom edges. Wax the case sides and runners too.

NK Assembly

This is a seldom-seen drawer style developed in the early 1900s by a Swedish manufacturer, Nordiska Kompaniet. It's called, oddly enough, the NK (pronounced "enco") drawer. It is quite different from a standard drawer.

The drawer box, except for the front, is slightly narrower than the drawer pocket. It is mounted atop a bottom assembly consisting of two low, wide slides and a plywood panel. The slides rest on the web frame and their edges bear against the case sides. Because the drawer sides are positioned about $1/16$" shy of the slide edges, they don't touch the case sides.

Thus the NK drawer has four advantages over standard drawers:

• The slides provide extra surface area right where it's needed, under the drawer.

• The slides reduce the amount of surface area rubbing at the sides (where it's not needed) to a smooth-running $1/2$".

• The bottom assembly can be trimmed and fit to the drawer opening before being attached to the rest of the drawer. This is much easier than fitting a standard drawer, especially for large drawers. Without the front, sides, and back of the drawer to obstruct your view, you can easily see where the bottom is binding.

• Because the drawer bottom sits proud of the drawer sides, there is no pressure to glue up an exactly square drawer box.

It's different, but not dramatically so. In NK construction, the drawer bottom — consisting of two low, wide runners and a bottom panel — is fitted to the drawer pocket. The drawer box is built separately and joined to the bottom. The resulting drawer is all wood, operates smoothly and fits perfectly.

A wide runner is the critical feature of the NK drawer. It's offset less than $1/8$" from the face of the drawer side, but that's enough to keep the side from dragging on the case side, so the drawer is easier to open and close. The runner's width distributes the drawer's weight over a broader area, reducing wear.

Make the Bottom Assembly

The bottom assembly is constructed and fitted to the drawer opening before the drawer box is even started.

Typically, the slides for NK drawers are $1/2$" high and 1" wide. They extend from the inner face of the drawer front to the case back. To get the slide length, simply subtract the drawer front thickness from the front-to-back dimension of the drawer pocket. And unless you're okay with the drawer banging against the case back, you should subtract about $1/4$" from the slide's length for clearance. (Glue closing stops to the drawer divider after the drawers are completed.)

Rabbet the slides for the bottom panel. The rabbet's shoulder should be centered under the drawer side. If the offset of the side is to be $1/16$" and the side is $1/2$" thick,

the rabbet should be $11/16$" wide (1" slide width minus $1/16$" offset minus half the side's thickness or $1/4$").

With the slides in the drawer opening, measure between the rabbet shoulders to determine the width of the bottom panel. The panel length is $1/4$" greater than the slide length, because it projects into a groove in the drawer front.

Cut the bottom panel, set it into the rabbets, and make sure the parts are square to the opening. The front ends of the slides should be the same distance from the drawer divider's edge. The plywood should project $1/4$" beyond the front ends of the slides. A snug or even tight fit is good; you can glue the parts together and then do a little hand-planing to achieve the perfect final fit.

Put the slides in their drawer pocket and measure from one to the other to determine the width of the plywood bottom panel. The panel should fit very tight; you ease the fit after gluing up the slides and panel.

Make the slides from a smooth, hard wood — hard maple in this case. Mill strips $1/2$" thick and 1" wide, then cut a rabbet $5/8$" wide and exactly as deep as the bottom panel thickness. I chamfer the bottom outside corner.

A good way to clamp the parts uses the case. Apply the glue and assemble the parts inside the drawer opening. Set cauls on the bottom panel edges, then wedge sticks between the cauls and the slides above them.

After the glue has set, complete the fitting. Plane the edges of the slides as needed to get the assembly gliding smoothly in and out of the case.

Cut the Drawer Box Parts

The drawer box consists of the front, sides and back. You cut the joints and assemble the box. Only then do you mate it to the bottom assembly.

The first task is fitting the front to the drawer pocket opening. Rip and crosscut the rough blank, then hand-plane the edges and ends in sequence to achieve that snug fit in the drawer opening.

The next task is to cut a groove for the plywood bottom panel. The panel fits into the groove and the ends of the slides butt against the front's inner face. It's important structurally and aesthetically for the groove to be blind, that is, stopped short of either end of the front. Accuracy here is pivotal to the alignment of the drawer front and the bottom assembly.

Rout the groove on the router table or with a plunge router and edge guide. You can square the ends of the groove with a chisel, or round off the plywood bottom panel's projecting edges. When you're done, test fit the front to the bottom assembly to ensure it aligns laterally.

Cut the sides and back. Measure from the top of the groove to the top of the drawer front. This is the width of both the sides and the back. Rip them to width, but when you crosscut them, leave them several inches long (including the back).

TOP RIGHT   Rout a stopped groove in the drawer front for the leading edge of the bottom panel. Measure in from the ends of the drawer and mark the groove's beginning and ending points on the face. On the fence, mark the tangents of the bit.

MIDDLE RIGHT   Check the fit of the bottom to the drawer front. The joint is an important part of the connection between the bottom assembly and the drawer box, so the fit must be snug.

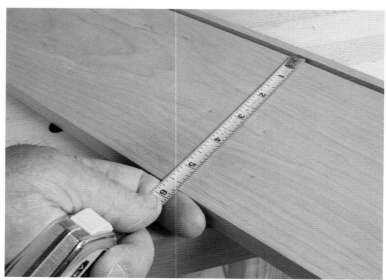

BOTTOM RIGHT   Determine the height of the drawer sides and back by measuring the drawer front from the groove to the side's top edge.

Cut the Joinery

Because the side-to-front joint must be stopped $^1/_2$" from the front's bottom edge, most machine-cut joints — like a lock joint, for example — won't work. You can rout a stopped rabbet and square the cut's end. Reinforce it with nails or brads or dowels.

The best joinery choice is half-blind dovetails, cut either with saw and chisels or with router and dovetail jig. Cut the sockets for the tails $^1/_{16}$" deeper than the side thickness. This recesses the side so it'll be clear of the case side. No friction.

A work-around is to use an applied front. Build a drawer box, attach it to the bottom assembly, then attach a show front. I wouldn't use this construction in fine furniture, but it would be acceptable in a built-in, kitchen cabinetry or other workaday cabinet or cupboard. Better you should learn to do dovetails.

Dry fit the sides to the front and the open-backed (for now) drawer box on its bottom assembly. Use this opportunity to establish the length of the sides and of the back. Determine the length of the back by measuring — just at the front — from the outside of one side to the outside of the other. Mark the sides along the back edges of the slides.

Dismantle the drawer, trim the sides to length and cut the drawer back. Cut and test-fit the sides-to-back joinery.

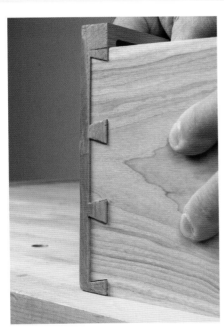

Clearance between the drawer sides and the case sides is the essence of smooth action with NK construction. The drawer front should fit snugly to the drawer pocket, and the sides should be recessed in the ends of the front $^1/_{16}$" to $^1/_8$". Dry fit each side-to-front joint to ensure you have that recess.

With the sides and front dry assembled, fit the bottom in place. Make sure — once again — that the bottom panel fits the groove and aligns properly side to side. Make sure the sides line up on the runners.

You get the best results by cutting parts to fit as you build the drawer. With the sides and front assembled dry, measure from side to side (FAR LEFT) to determine the length of the back (adjust the measurement to accommodate the joinery you intend to use at the back). Fit the bottom in place and mark the sides for length (LEFT).

Assemble the Drawer

Before gluing up the drawer, do one last dry assembly. The drawer front should center perfectly on the bottom, its ends flush with the drawer slides. The back should also be centered on the bottom assembly, with the sides parallel to the slides. Worry this detail now, when there's no glue setting and you can take your time. Get the box square and centered on the bottom. Then drill a hole though the bottom panel into the drawer back. During the glue-up, drive a dowel into the hole, forcing the assembly into alignment.

Apply glue to the dovetails now, and assemble the drawer box. Clamp the box, but continue with the assembly. Apply glue to the bottom edges of the drawer box and to the groove in the drawer front. Join the bottom assembly to the box. Make sure the ends of the front align properly with the slides. Drive a dowel into the registration hole. Clamp the bottom and box and set the drawer aside until the glue sets.

When the clamps are off, check the drawer's fit. It's not unusual for a bit of work with a hand plane to be needed to achieve a smooth-sliding fit.

Finally, pare the dovetail pins flush with the drawer sides. Try using a plane iron on this task rather than a chisel. If you pare too deeply with a chisel, the end grain can crumble, marring the appearance of the joint. Instead, stack index cards beside the pin — all but flush with top — and make light shearing cuts. Remove a couple of cards and pare some more. Keep up the routine until the pins are flush with the drawer sides.

ABOVE Begin final assembly with the drawer upside down. Apply glue to the edges of sides and back, and on the projecting edge of the bottom panel. Slide the bottom into place, align it, and apply clamps to hold the bottom against the front.

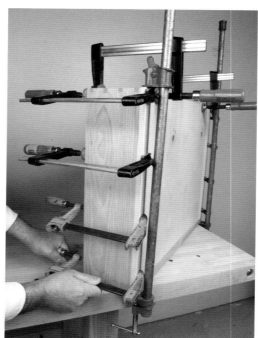

LEFT Tip the drawer up, standing it on blocks or at a corner of the bench. Apply clamps to seat the bottom against the drawer's edges.

BELOW Pare the protruding pins flush with the sides. Depending upon the amount of material to be trimmed, you can begin with a chisel, then switch to a chisel plane. You can leave the half-pins at the top and bottom, or square them.

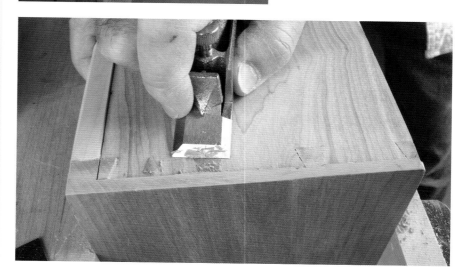

A Production Drawer

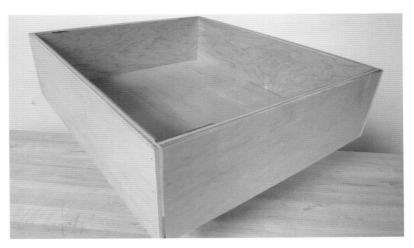

Not every project merits custom-fitted drawers. Many a project calls for lots of strong, reasonably attractive drawers but doesn't allow time for painstakingly sizing, assembling and fitting them one-at-a-time. These projects are on tight schedules and usually on tight budgets.

Every production cabinetmaker has a method for building such drawers — pocket-screw joinery in plywood, glued-and-screwed butt joints in MCP (melamine coated particleboard). Outsourcing is increasingly popular. You can buy drawer boxes constructed to your specifications, delivered knocked down or already assembled.

I prefer to make my own drawers, using a streamlined construction routine. The first order of business is to decide which manufactured slide I'm going to use because that may affect dimensions and the distance the bottom must be recessed. I make a cut list. I already know what joinery I'm going to use, though not necessarily what materials.

If a finish is required, I'll use pre-finished plywood — 1/2" for the box walls and 1/4" for the bottom. The benefit is a tough, stink-free finish without a finishing step. If a finish isn't required, I'll use 1/2" Baltic birch for the walls, 1/4" birch for the bottom.

If exposed plywood edges are acceptable, I'll plan to chamfer or slightly round the top edges. If not, I'll have to include an edge-banding operation in the routine.

With the material and a cutting list in hand, producing stacks of sides, fronts, backs and bottoms doesn't take long. Use an ATB (alternate top bevel) blade with 60 to 80 teeth, a zero-clearance insert and position stops to knock out uniform, chip-free parts.

ABOVE Here's an all-purpose drawer that's attractive, strong, and durable. Mount it on manufactured slides, apply a front, and install it in a kitchen or bath, family room or office, workshop or storeroom.

LEFT Don't count on a plywood sheet having straight edges or being square. Your first cut should establish a straight edge; use it as the reference edge to rip the sheet into strips of the required widths.

BELOW Crosscut the strips into sides, fronts and backs. Use a reliable miter gauge or cutoff box with a stop to ensure the crosscuts are square and like parts are uniformly sized.

Cut the Joints and Assemble

The drawer is assembled with glued and nailed rabbets. The rabbets are cut in the sides, so they overlap and conceal the ends of the front and back. The bottom is housed in grooves cut in the sides and front, and fastened to the back; it can be glued or not, as you prefer.

Cut the grooves for the drawer bottom as the first joinery operation. Use a $^7/_{32}$" slot cutter in a router table, with the cutter elevated appropriately for whatever bottom recess is required for your slides. Set the fence to limit the groove depth to about $^3/_{16}$".

If you have a second router table — I do — you can set it up with a chamfer or round-over bit and ease the top edges of sides, fronts and backs.

Cut the rabbets next. The table saw with a dado cutter is fast and accurate.

After sanding the parts, assemble the boxes. Swipe some glue on the rabbets, press the parts together firmly, and fire in the fasteners. Before the glue sets, slide the bottom into its grooves, seat it to force the drawer into square (if it isn't already) and fasten it to the back. Drawer's done.

The dimensions of the drawers don't change any of the setups. You can move through any assortment of parts widths and lengths without interruption, because the reference surfaces for the cuts are ends and edges.

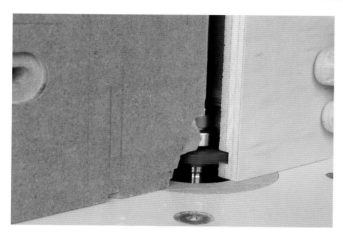

Set up a router table with a $^7/_{32}$" slot cutter, adjusted to make a $^3/_{16}$"-deep groove. The offset of the groove from the box's bottom edge is usually dictated by the type and model of slide being used. Rout through grooves in fronts and sides.

Cut rabbets in the ends of the drawer sides on the table saw with a dado cutter.

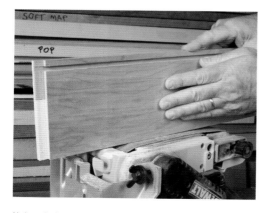

Unbanded exposed edges — the top edges, in other words — should be sanded to present the best appearance (LEFT). An edge sander isn't essential; I upend a portable belt sander and clamp it to the bench. A narrow chamfer routed on each edge completes the cosmetic treatment (RIGHT).

Apply a thin coat of glue to the rabbets and assemble the sides, front and back. The bottom helps hold the parts in alignment as you pull a joint tight and fire two or three 1" brads into it.

Mounting Applied Fronts

Applied fronts are used on all sorts of furniture, including kitchen cabinets. Mounting them isn't all that difficult. The job is best tackled after the drawers have been installed in the case.

The applied fronts used on factory-built frameless kitchen cabinets are usually mounted using eccentric adjusters. The cabinets ship with the fronts already mounted. The adjusters allow the installer to tweak the alignment of a drawer front without removing it.

My own preference with built-ins is to wait until after cabinet is installed — all shimmed and leveled and screwed to the wall — before attaching the drawer fronts. But I'm not working on the clock; I'm never going to be the first one done, but I always endeavor to do the job just a little better than the other guy.

However you approach the job, the key to visual satisfaction is alignment. Whether you are attaching fronts to frameless cabinetry or a studio furniture piece, your goal is a narrow, consistent gap all around the drawer front. The best trick to fulfilling the goal is to use shims to set and hold that gap between drawer fronts and whatever frames them — posts, rails or drawer dividers.

I usually use small pieces of plastic laminate (Formica), but I know folks who use pocket change (nickels, pennies, and dimes in diminishing order of thickness).

In a nutshell, you start at the bottom, setting the front on shims and aligning it evenly between the posts. Clamp it to the drawer box. Remove the drawer to drive mounting screws through the structural front into the applied front. Work your way up from the bottom, always using the same shims between the new front and the one below it.

LEFT Measure the fronts of the drawer boxes, individually and collectively, to determine the width of each drawer front. Though clearance between drawer fronts is essential, it's best to create it as you mount them.

BELOW Shims are the key to aligning and spacing the drawer fronts. With all but the bottom two drawer boxes removed from the case, set the bottom drawer's front on a pair of shims. Using a shim, check the clearance between the top of the front and the drawer box above it.

ABOVE When you are satisfied with the fit, remove the upper drawer box and clamp the drawer front to the bottom box. Make sure the clearances at the ends of the drawer front are equal.

LEFT Remove the drawer from the case. Drill pilot holes and drive mounting screws. Washer head screws (INSET) are dandy for this job. The number of screws needed varies with the width and height of the drawer front. I used four for this 9" x 25" front.

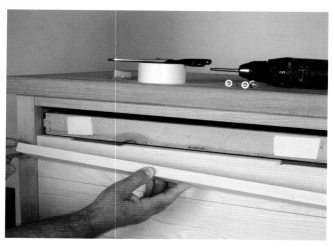

Repeat the process to mount the next higher drawer front. Mount the bottom drawer on its slides, as well as the two drawer boxes above it. Rest the next drawer front on shims atop the front immediately below. Check the clearance between the front and the box above it. When it's right, remove the top box and clamp the front to its box.

Carpet tape is the solution where you don't have access for regular clamps. The situation is common at the top of a bank of drawers. After fitting the drawer front, apply a couple of patches of double-sided tape to the drawer box and press the drawer front firmly against them. (Make some provision for opening the drawer, of course!) The tape will hold the front while you open the drawer and drive the mounting screws.

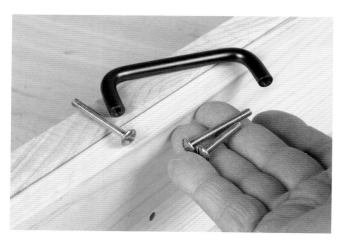

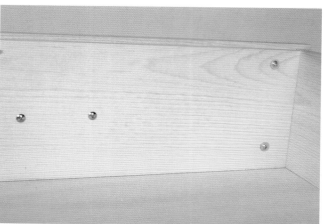

Drawer fronts mounted, lay out and drill holes for mounting the pulls. Pulls are typically packaged with the required number of screws, which are too short to penetrate both structural and applied fronts. Buy longer replacements. In the end, the front is secured with six screws — a wood screw in each corner and a pair in the center that mount the pull.

A uniform gap around each drawer front is the ultimate goal.

SUPPLIERS

**ADAMS & KENNEDY —
THE WOOD SOURCE**
6178 Mitch Owen Rd.
P.O. Box 700
Manotick, ON
Canada K4M 1A6
613-822-6800
www.wood-source.com
Wood supply

ADJUSTABLE CLAMP COMPANY
404 N. Armour St.
Chicago, IL 60622
312-666-0640
www.adjustableclamp.com
Clamps and woodworking tools

THE BURGESS EDGE
Michael Burgess
P.O. Box 32 Route 125
Ripton, Vermont 05766
802.233.1489
www.burgessedge.com
*A revolutionary edge-banding
system using specially designed
router bits*

B&Q
Portswood House
1 Hampshire Corporate Park
Chandlers Ford
Eastleigh
Hampshire, England SO53
3YX
0845 609 6688
www.diy.com
*Woodworking tools, supplies
and hardware*

BUSY BEE TOOLS
130 Great Gulf Dr.
Concord, ON
Canada L4K 5W1
1-800-461-2879
www.busybeetools.com
Woodworking tools and supplies

**CONSTANTINE'S WOOD CENTER
OF FLORIDA**
1040 E. Oakland Park Blvd.
Fort Lauderdale, FL 33334
800-443-9667
www.constantines.com
Tools, woods, veneers, hardware

**FRANK PAXTON LUMBER
COMPANY**
5701 W. 66th St.
Chicago, IL 60638
800-323-2203
www.paxtonwood.com
Wood, hardware, tools, books

THE HOME DEPOT
2455 Paces Ferry Rd. NW
Atlanta, GA 30339
800-430-3376 (U.S.)
800-628-0525 (Canada)
www.homedepot.com
*Woodworking tools, supplies
and hardware*

KLINGSPOR ABRASIVES INC.
2555 Tate Blvd. SE
Hickory, N.C. 28602
800-645-5555
www.klingspor.com
Sandpaper of all kinds

LEE VALLEY TOOLS LTD.
P.O. Box 1780
Ogdensburg, NY 13669-6780
800-871-8158 (U.S.)
800-267-8767 (Canada)
www.leevalley.com
*Woodworking tools and
hardware*

LOWE'S COMPANIES, INC.
P.O. Box 1111
North Wilkesboro, NC 28656
800-445-6937
www.lowes.com
*Woodworking tools, supplies
and hardware*

**ROCKLER WOODWORKING AND
HARDWARE**
4365 Willow Dr.
Medina, MN 55340
800-279-4441
www.rockler.com
*Woodworking tools, hardware
and books*

**TREND MACHINERY & CUTTING
TOOLS LTD.**
Odhams Trading Estate
St. Albans Rd.
Watford
Hertfordshire, U.K.
WD24 7TR
01923 224657
www.trendmachinery.co.uk
*Woodworking tools and
hardware*

WATERLOX COATINGS
908 Meech Ave.
Cleveland, OH 44105
800-321-0377
www.waterlox.com
Finishing supplies

WOODCRAFT SUPPLY LLC
1177 Rosemar Rd.
P.O. Box 1686
Parkersburg, WV 26102
800-535-4482
www.woodcraft.com
Woodworking hardware

WOODWORKER'S HARDWARE
P.O. Box 180
Sauk Rapids, MN 56379-0180
800-383-0130
www.wwhardware.com
Woodworking hardware

WOODWORKER'S SUPPLY
1108 N. Glenn Rd.
Casper, WY 82601
800-645-9292
www.woodworker.com
*Woodworking tools and
accessories, finishing supplies,
books and plans*

More great titles from Popular Woodworking!

BILL HYLTON'S FRAME & PANEL MAGIC

By Bill Hylton

Whether you're a first-time woodworker or a seasoned pro, you will immediately transform the way you build everything. Frame-and-panel doors and cabinet sides are your ticket to building projects that are stronger, more attractive and impervious to the seasonal expansion and contraction of solid wood.

ISBN 13: 978-1-55870-740-5
ISBN 10: 1-55870-740-9
paperback, 128 p., #70693

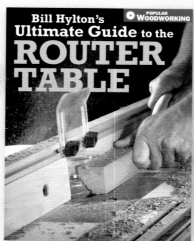

ISBN 13: 978-1-55870-796-2
ISBN 10: 1-55870-796-4
paperback, 128 p., # Z0595

BILL HYLTON'S ULTIMATE GUIDE TO THE ROUTER

By Bill Hylton

The router table opens up a whole new world of using the router that simply can't be done using it any other way. You'll be shown how to edge profile, make moulding, cut lock-miter joints, box joints, rabbets, grooves, splined miters, use templates, pin rout and more!

FINE FURNITURE FOR A LIFETIME

By Glen Huey

This book provides easy-to-follow instruction and step-by-step photos for ten exciting projects inspired by 18th- and 19th-century designs. You'll learn how to master mortise-and-tenon joinery, dovetailed drawers and other great techniques for handcrafting gorgeous pieces with classic lines and solid construction.

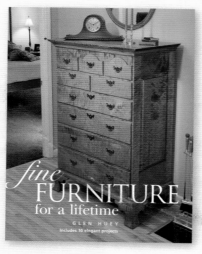

ISBN 13: 978-1-55870-593-7
ISBN 10: 1-55870-593-7
paperback, 128 p., #70533

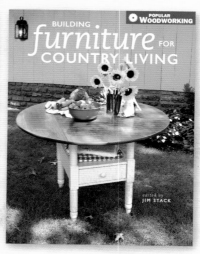

ISBN 13: 978-1-55870-788-7
ISBN 10: 1-55870-788-3
paperback, 128 p., # Z0489

BUILDING FURNITURE FOR COUNTRY LIVING

Edited by Jim Stack

Nothing conveys the comfort and warmth of hearth and home quite like handmade, solid wood furniture. We've assembled a collection of "comfort" furniture for your home. By following the detailed step-by-step instruction and photos, you too can bring the comfort of country living into your home, no matter what your skill level.

These and other great woodworking books are available at your local bookstore, woodworking stores or from online suppliers.

www.popularwoodworking.com